UNIVERSAL WISDOM

UNIVERSAL WISDOM

Pearls of Divine Guidance

Vennelakanti Prakasam

Divine Humanism Trust

To
My Parents

V. Narayana Rao, For Intellection
VenkataLakshmamma, for Interlocution

Acknowledgment

I wish to specially thank Mr Rapuru Sridhar Reddy and Mahendrada Sairamprasad for helping me in the preparation of the manuscript.

Prologue

ithout understanding there will be no comprehension. Without comprehension faith is just faith. We should get to know about things we don't know and till then we have to wait. We should not give lectures. If we don't understand the meaning of the word God, meaning of the word Soul (Atma) and if we don't know all the details regarding Avatar(Incarnation) and rebirth (punarjanma), better we read the necessary literature, and listen to preachers. But we have to wait till comprehension has taken place. We can do all the worshipping rituals as part of family culture.We can visit places of worship. We can celebrate festivals but we should not give lectures under the illusion of knowledge.

We should first think about things which we can easily understand. Comprehension takes place only with lot of hard thinking. It is our comprehension which becomes our guide. Don't get into trouble by arguing with your coevals. Don't you ever act as if you are a great knower. If there is God he cannot be a nepotist. Caste, religious denomination, race, complexion and country of birth will not be a consideration for salvation or rejection of it. Does salvation mean going to a pleasure dome? If the Lord of the Heaven is God our entry should be our praxis but not our socio-religious identity. Heaven is a place of bliss and it will bless us on the basis of our actions. If our earning is unacceptable and if our actions are unacceptable God will not give us any concession.

Our life style while alive and our post-life style will be same. This post-life state is called mukti (liberation), which interestingly can be achieved right here and now. To effect the state we need to follow five basic principles. If we wear that garland of five principles with us they will operate as restraining chains keeping us away from sins and also as five boating streams to reach the right destination. The first principle is **Socialness.** The second principle is **Dutifulness**. The third principle is **Love**. The fourth principle is **Forgiveness**. The fifth principle is **Compassion.** These five principles dovetail themselves and guide us to Mukti (salvation). The Epilogue will elucidate it further.

UNIVERSAL WISDOM

Pearls of Divine Guidance

1 Dharma is societal, but beyond sentiment,
   Dharma is situational,but beyond bias,
   Dharma is age-driven, but accords with higher truth.

2. Justice is a reflection of virtue and fairplay,
   Justice transcends self-and-other difference,
   Justice adapts to circumstances reflecting values.

3. The individual is a soloist but central for society,
   Society is groupismic,but is central for culture,
   Culture is collectivist, but is central for living.

4. Duty management is essential and ethical,
   Good is practicable always for everyone,
   What divides people and harms is unworthy.

5. The antidote to 'I', 'me' and 'my' is 'we', 'us' and 'our',
   The antidote to anger is forgiving calmness,
   The antidote to pollution is clarifying truth.

6. The real word is meaning -- heavy,
   True worship is devotion – heavy,
   The real food is nutrition –heavy.

7. Greed is the most painful disorder,
   Anger is a very painful emotion,
   Ignorance is the most painful grief.

8. Measure yourself well to suit societal norms,
   Customize your good intentions to suit social needs,
   Cultivate what you think of to effect right form and
      substance. .

                                   Vennelakanti Prakasam

9. Distribute appropriate remuneration for work,
    Treat labour theft as a serious social sin,
    Increase the reward of labour over time.

10. Treat others as your own kinsmen,
    Give what you can when asked for,
    Speak kindly and satisfy them.

11. Perceptual awareness leads to comprehension,
    Erasure of self-other distinction leads to relationship,
    Maintaing time and relationships leads to peace and
        comfort.

12. Sharing mindset and sense of service ensure growth,
    Commitment to duty management ensures growth,
    Pondering over social welfare ensures growth.

13. The needs of mankind are of supreme importance,
    Worthy of grasping, remembering and executing.
    Fullfilling others' needs accords to Divinity.

14. The heat of falsehood dries us up,
    The flame of deceit will burn us down,
    Ego and ignorance make us invalids.

15. Pride and conceit are the traits of the weak,
    Haste and harshness are traits of the timid,
    Patience, forgiveness, and love are traits of the
        strong.

16. Understand if perceived and follow if favorable,
    Do not slight the others with the illusion of knowing,
    Keep your words clear and avoid deceitful
        doublespeak.

17. If confident, you are like Narayana,
    Selfishness if excessive you are Naraka,
    Recognise your limits, Cognise the Divine within
        you.

18. Planets effect the nature of the brain,
    Experiential education is our livelihood,
    Everything is possible if there is transparent effort.

19. What tickles you is the seed for your action,
    Total sincerity and commitment will be the
        investment,
    The real income is what benefits you and others.

20. The concept should be strengthened by ideation,
    Ideation should be followed by serious reflection,
    Praxis should be for the welfare of the community.

21. Look, hear, comprehend, concentrate,
    Achieve the intended goal with assiduity,
    But work should not be just for one's own self.

22. With 'a' take a look and observe,
    With 'u' yearn for excellence,
    With 'm', show ingenuity, **Aum** is divinity.

23. Patience helps to soothe the mind,
    Skill is the actual key to success,
    Generosity is a testament to true devotion.

24. Let not the weed of desire distrub duty management,
    Let not harshness distrub the value of your words,
    Let not false sweetness creep into your statement.

25. Forsake inaction, adopt right action,
    Immobility is negative,calmness is positive,
    Feed the cattle, dont become rich rattle.

26. Temperance is the antidote to tragedy,
    Sobriety is the key to good relationship,
    The way to liberation is freedom from anger.

27. Do not lie for self-gain or for others' loss,
    For self-defence and protection don't crib to fib,
    Shun selfishness and strive for general good.

28. Directionlessness and stubbornness will make you a
        loner,
    Hostility and lascivousness will lead you to enmity,
    Nature and nurture will effect socialness and harmony.

29. Time management and relationship govern life journey,
    Be pragmatic by focusing on right activity,
    With methodicity you can achieve elevation.

30. There are no clans for the seeds, fields and the soul,
    The clans are only for mundane social identities,
    Virtues and good deeds are cosmic and transcendental.

31. No flamboyance in the matters of charity,
     Don't you ever forget what you get from others,
     There is no expiation for ingratitude and impudence.

32. Mother, Father, Teacher, God merge in Avadhuta,
     That Mendicant-Saint will guide you, be with him
         totally,
     The real Guru is your Ciceroni, guiding,mentoring
         and tutoring.

33. The wise man does not vacuously blame others,
     Reading strengthens the process of our intellection,
     Position is for helpful service, not to unleash authority.

34. Cognition and intellection are the best of all activities,
     Ignorance, anger, and greed are terrifying of all states,
     Wisdom, gentleness,and sacrifice are pleasant mindsets.

35. The basis of cognition is the milk of experience,
     Doctrine is the staff, intelligence is the cord,
     What you get with churning is butter 555.

36. Knowledge brooks no caste, creed or region
         differences,
     Love for one and all in engendered by knowledge,
     Love leads to forgiveness, forgiveness leads to happiness.

37. Fib not cognizance, fear not ignorance,
     Know comprehensively and share with the seeker,
     Respect wisdom and encourage the learned.

                                    Vennelakanti Prakasam

38. Skill is commendable, knowledge is real wealth,
    Health is the real benefit, satisfaction is the real pleasure,
    True devotion is the service rendered and selfless
       thinking.

39. You are more important than your family and clan,
    The transcending of dualities is above all else,
    Altruistic services are indeed sattvic and Divine.

40. Unfortunate that if haves behave like have-nots,
    Satiation with what you have is plenitude,
    Real having is actually sharing with others.

41. Prohibition of malice, exuberance of prescience,
    Gloating is forbidden, and secret donation is in order,
    Earn righteously, spend methodically which is virtue.

42. Blessed are those who are humble and meek,but not
       sleek,
    Blessed are those who admit their mistakes and
       correct them,
    Blessed are those who guide, who help and who forgive.

43. Don't you ever feast with labour theft,
    Labor thief is a parasite on the society,
    Make the worker reasonably happy.

44. Virtue must avoid the company of evil and harm,
    Virtue must grow in speech and give refuge to the
       needy,
    Virtue is the guiding path to contentment and
       liberation.

45. Let go of hatred before prayer,
    Let go of greed before the offering,
    Let go of competitiveness before preaching.

46. Experiencing pleasures in the right way is a virtue,
    Fear and deceit are not to be weapons and shields,
    Achieving social welfare is the true salvation.

47. Your faith is important, not luxurious rituals,
    Faith needs a foundation for progress, not foolishness,
    Wisdom should show real light and should not lead
        to pride.

48. Heaven and hell are beyond caste,creed and code,
    Hell is for doing things that should not be done,
    Heaven is for doing deeds that need and deserve to
        be done.

49. What you think is yours and what you do is yours,
    Not at all important, what you are and whose you
        are,
    You are what you think and what you do,verily so.

50. Official partiality is akin to paralysis,
    Dealing with responsibilities is the right thing,
    Doing good to many is the true Yajna.

51. Your work should not be theft of others' things,
    Your work should not be related to violence,
    Your work should not end till your breath meets its
        end.

52. If the Atma is us, then the society is Paramatma,
Power if it is our good, devotion if it is social good,
That is true emancipation for our life journey.

53. Your prosperity should benefit many people,
Your wisdom should enlighten many a mind,
Your exhortations should illuminate all the races.

54. Need for vision is a weapon of philanthropy,
Your wealth should become investment for others,
Your appreciative generosity is indeed altruism.

55. Sinful it is to secretly do what is contrary to nature,
Natural it is the virtue that comforts the poor,
Functioning for others beyond dualities is Divinity.

56. Legends, counterlegends are beyond logic,
They are just indices to the history of human survival,
Remember what is known, learn what is neoteric.

57. The righteousness and agape are the best,
Do not suffer from ego and do not tremble with fear,
Reach out to many with love and move forward with
     courage.

58. Do not take credit for someone else's work,
Do not blame others for your mistake,
Love and kindness are every being's right.

59. Keep your body always in good health,
Keep your mind all the time in active mood,
Keep your sense of duty as of great value.

60. Love, forgiveness,compassion, socialness and
        dutifulness,
    Enjoy treading elegantly this five fold path of
        Effulgence,
    Only then Jeevanmukti the liberating emancipation
        is yours.

61. Without the mother you won't be, and without wife
        you cannot sire,
    No daughters-in-law, no grandfathers, no great-
        grandfathers,
    Know the value of the mothering person and act
        gracefully.

62. Familiality establishes validity for begetting and
        bearing,
    Wedlock is loveship going beyond friendship,
    Offspring well-being is a testament to your existence.

63. Manmatha's parents were Lakshmi and Narayana,
    Their serpentine bedstead is their spousal couch,
    Human couples remember reflect the Divine spousality.

64. The bond of Saraswati and Brahma is one of satvic
        cognition,
    Ideating and wording should be in the right direction,
    Sounding guidance to the whole of livingdom.

65. The Two in One Shiva and Parvati are worldly forces,
    The hint is to run the ship together no matter what,
    Internal closeness, external distancing are all in one.

66. Hear the good in whatever is said and uttered,
    Share with others the valuable in what you think of,
    What is conceived and what is shared should be the
        same.

67. Temple, school and wealth should be accessible to all,
    Healing, education, food are the need for all,
    The value of courtesy is essential for everyone.

68. A benevolent usurer is better than a greedy educated
        man,
    Skilled workman is far better than half knowing
        teacher,
    Gentle ascetics are better than warring couples.

69. Worship is a work that brings good to others,
    Worship done for selfish ends is useless,
    Game if others can watch, song if others can listen.

70. Go beyond yourself and do goodness to all,
    Put on frowning face to instill discipline in children,
    Be content with what you have and crave not for the
        unhad.

71. Ethic knows no gender distinction,nor does the
        epidemic,
    Hunger makes no distinction between the rich and
        the poor,
    Goodness brooks no distinction between the self and
        the other.

72. Do good with the mind, lead with the will,
Intellect your ideation and share the results,
Enjoy with others the honey of your experience.

73. Your sight is yours, your lip is yours, your smile is yours,
Your mind is yours, your words are yours, your
hands are yours,
Your wealth is not yours though, your status is not
yours though.

74. Weigh your speech, ensure your dignity,
Kink not, lest you shold sink,
Be sharp at work but not belligerent.

75. Immortality is impossible, pursue it not,
Righteousness is likely, pursue it,
Jeevanmukti is possible on the path of Dharma.

76. Wisdom is not possible without logic,
Peace is not possible without endurance,
Salvation is not possible without satiating.

77. Divinity does not come close unless charity is the
in-thing,
Mukti doesn't mark you without equanimity,
Happiness has no case without love as the base.

78. Work according to the verve, reward according to work,
Nourishment should be the same for one and all,
Care, love and respect should ensure health of
psychosoma.

   Vennelakanti Prakasam

79. Do not suspect and criticize baselessly,
    In other's words take the stuff, discard the chaff,
    Note it, your ideation is of paramount importance.

80. Smile on the lip, gentleness in speaking,
    With gentleness everything will be cool and smooth,
    Character is charm for erudition, charity is charm
        for richness.

81. Devotion for food yields no fruition,
    Diligence at work gives energy and synergy,
    Equanimity yields real salvation right here.

82. Attention is the base for cropping, cooking and
        couching,
    Thorough knowledge of the work should keep
        company,
    Love for everything and concern for everyone are a
        must.

83. The village goddesses are the basis of our social being,
    The source of our growth is the living gods, the
        parents,
    Gurus open the paths and the Inner Light leads us
        forward.

84. The wise uphold others in the path of knowledge,
    Karmayogi strengthens others on the path of
        Dutifulness,
    The Saint-Soldier form will make us all invincible.

85. No untruthful love and no unpleasant truth,
Pleasant truth is ineed the true weapon,
Silence is the shield when no other choice.

86. Knowledge is superior to sacrifices and rituals,
Wisdom engenders sympathetic social
    consciousness,
The philosophy of the Sant-Sipahi is great in all
    respects.

87. Shun laziness and be self sufficient,
Unworthy subject and wrong logic do not fit in,
Violence and false testimony are inappropriate.

88. Profiteers and tax evaders are malefactors,
Sinful it is to do wrong things secretly,
Help the humble, stop blaming wrongly.

89. All races,all nations and all religions are one,
Trees, livestock, all kinds of animals and water beings,
There is no denying they have the same right over
    nature.

90. Look at the dog, the elephant, the cow as one,
Look at the fruit eater and dog eater as one,
Promote the right value for each task and cheer up.

91. All fruits are from the hard worker,
Blessed are those who bring them to us,
The ones who cook are the real breadgivers.

92. Cooperation is the way to heaven and vengeance is
        the way to hell,
     Equality is the path to peace, arrogance is the path to
        the enmity,
     Forbearce leads to contentment, contentment leads
        to liberation.

93. Do not quarrel about the atma and paramatma,
     Social welfare is the union of the individual and the
        society,
     Helping others is the first step, ensuring equality is
        the final step.

94. Fasten selfishness with a chain to the window,
     Reduce the pungency of anger with sweetness of love,
     Think 'all I's are me' and that is real consciousness.

95. The base for virtue is righteousness,
     The base for task management is the feeling of 'ours',
     ' Me' should lead to 'us', ' let us' leading further to ' let's'

96. Telling truth is better than being quiet,
     Mental chanting is better than oral chanting,
     Commiting to social purpose is better than
        self-consecration.

97. Steadfastness is overcoming of pleasures and sorrows,
     Steadfastness is for stunning the senses and doing
        right actions,
     Steadfastness is for the general good, brushing aside
        personal good.

98. Share knowledge systematically with those who
     seek it,
     Keep away glitz and ritz, achive equanimity,
     Knowledge distributed humbly grows nimbly.

99. Discerning concern and selfless service for parents
     is a must,
     Humility and feeling of gratitude to the teachers is
     a must,
     Affection for others and equality for all is a must.

100. Don't bubble up for compliments, don't show off
      the shown value,
      Do not get discouraged by negativity and do not
      crumble if ignored,
      Enjoy the satisfaction of achieving proper duty
      management.

101. Slide not sideways to get money,
      Control the senses seeking intoxication,
      Notice the wrong turn and return the mind to the
      right path.

102. Observe the needs of the companions,
      Go forward to help others to the extent you can,
      Don't ignore the needs of your own people.

103. Don't pursue false preachers,
      Dont try to do useless work,
      Give up harmful tactics,choose right steps.

104. Seeking someone else's spouse is dangerous,
     The presence of thieves and thugs also is dangerous,
     Taking up wrong work and failing at it is also
     dangerous.

105. Absolute and acceptable truth is right,
     Unacceptable and false speech is wrong,
     Truth is path-showing and reality is object-based.

106. Honesty is important, no deception, not even a bit,
     Be diligent in what you are doing, don't take to
     shortcuts,
     The fee for entry into Heaven is righteous behaviour.

107. The seeker should be given as per our capacity
     Only then will come to us what is needed,
     Life is like 'give and take' 'take and give.'

108. Mastery in work, goodness in mind, restraint in
     behaviour fit in,
     Humility and affection in the service of the elders is
     welcome,
     Pretending to be angry to instill discipline is not
     unwelcome.

109. Sense is important to the word, sense is the source
     of knowledge,
     It is academic theft to claim someone else's word as
     your word,
     Recognise, compare, intellect and knowledge is the
     result.

110. Non-violence, neutrality, sensual control are
        asceticism,
     It is not acceptable to relinquish family responsibility,
     Mukti is about performing one's duty transcending
        dualities.

111. Energy and firmness provide us strength,
     Meanness and lust weaken the strength,
     Gratitude and impartiality enhance that strength.

112. Anger and greed can be controlled with the help of
        trust,
     For that we must have friends who are trustworthy,
     Goal-purity, self-confidence, and self-esteem are
        essential qualities.

113. There should be no selfishness in the giver,
     Propriety and altruism are very important,
     Seeing good work done, others follows suit.

114. Do not torture the unarmed, the submissive, the
        weak,
     Violence is abhorrent, inevitable retaliation
        justified,
     Love, forgiveness, and piety are very precious.

115. Enhance agape which is both weapon and shield,
     Practice all kinds of peace-giving forgiveness,
     Negating negativity, establish positivity in words.

116. The sage is distant for conflict and close to harmony,
      Only if necessary, show strength and negotiate
          peace,
      Both thought and speech should lead to productive
          alliance.

117. The witness should not be greedy, nor should he be
          immoral,
      Prejudice and ignorance are not appropriate for a
          judge
      It is important to share with others even if denying
          for the self a bit.

118. It is right to punish with words, slaps or fines,
      All can be used if necessary but not inappropriately,
      Punishment should lead to change in the
          offender,not rancour.

119. It is worthwhile to work on your own without
          burdening others,
      The woman fulfills the family responsibility with
          her own efficiency,
      Association with others should ensure appropriate
          behaviour.

120. Non-violence, truthfulness, abstinence are
          paramount,
      Counter violence, sometimes silence and if
          necessary negativity,
      Will be alright if inevitable for keeping life on its
          track.

121. Repentance, unblemished conduct lead to purity,
Penance and charity also are conducive to purity,
If all these are there, then we become exalted.

122. The value of education lies in comprehension and
intellection,
Selfless practitioners are better than the greedy
learned,
Activitiy for others' welfare excels all other acts.

123. Food should be given first to future mothers,
Next to guests and their followers,
Finally and happily to the hosting householders.

124. Without toil life will be strife,
The workaholic is the real doer,
Reward, value, good food are his right.

125. Hunting for occupation or training may be
unavoidable,
Hunt not sleeping animals or feeding animals,
Injured animal should not be hunted and no
hunting for entertainment.

126. Recognize the consciousness that is in every being,
Note the consciousness that is all around,
Do not insult any creature, do not inflict
unwarranted hurt.

127. In some the consciousness radiates as Divinity,
Divinity should be given formidable value,
Accept them as Gurus if you vibrate well.

128. Identify the inspiring Divine Humans,
The Divine grace of Balarama laid the furrow for
agrifarming,
The Divine grace of Krishna laid the route to dairy
farming.

129. Going beyond terrestrial, aerial and aquatic beings,
The two Divine graces led to food prodcution with
farming,
The Divine brothers showed us knowledge path
bypassing rituals path.

130. Our nature and our actions decide our life,
Relying on Someone's grace is not felicitous,
Courage and perseverance are essential for doing
our duty,

131. Unrealized devotion cannot give salvation,
Awareness-driven action ensures success and
welfare,
Meditation facilitates self-improvement and
realization.

132. Our words, thoughts and wealth are weapons for
service,
Doting on God is of greater value than being with
God,
Doing hands are more important than promising
lips.

133. Determination can withstand any obstacle and
          impediment,
      Our reward is always achievable with hard work
          and patience,
      Listening, ruminating, and planning are the tools
          we need.

134. Divine intellection is stronger than ritual worship,
      With intellection we achive total comprehension,
      The real nature of people can be realized with
          intellection.

135. Proper belief is formed by intellection,
      Thought is weighty and more valuable than words,
      Only then the consciousness within us becomes
          Divine.

136. Love shown for an end is selfishness,
      Love shared with others is admirable,
      The love for righteousness is agape.

137. Divine consciousness is all pervading,
      Lifting the Hill is protecting us with knowledge,
      With Divine thinking we become Divine.

138. The same sermon provides a new vision,
      While doing one's duty, good not to worry about
          the result,
      Transcending the dualities, restrain the ephemeral
          body.

139. Get closer to the Supreme with self-exaltation,
     What the exalted do the others tend to follow,
     Grasp the truth, subdue the rest and become a role
          model.

140. Mind shows the path, intellect gives the grip,
     Conscience guides and reigns the senses,
     The soul binds desires to follow the divine path.

141. The source and substance are the same for all living
          things,
     Learn this basic point and use your common sense,
     Be prudent and move forward, do not be decived.

142. Differences are there in nature, nurture and culture,
     Differences are there in goals and modes of action,
     Difference should not be there in love and respect.

143. The scholar, the common man, the cow,
     The horse, the dog and the dog eater,
     Treats them all as equals the Enlightened one.

144. Knowledge is not for money and fun,
     Knowledge is the real light in action,
     Everything is possible with equanimity.

145. Purity outside and piety inside,
     A smiling face and a positive talk,
     The inner nature and the outer culture should be
          alike.

146. The Supreme Divine is realized differently by
        different people,
     Dote on your deity the known way,
     Be familiar with your prayer and worship.

147. Do not blaspheme any other doting process,
     The unknown are more than the known,
     The way you know is easy for you.

148. Ignorance leads to prejudice, ending with loathing,
     Self-esteem is the ability to balance things,
     It is illogical to ignore the all pervasive Chaitanya.

149. See all in you, you will be happy,
     Think of all in you, you will be satisified,
     Be happy with what you have and distribute the
        surplus.

150. Feel the well-being of others is your well-being,
     Strive well to see that others don't starve.
     That is the divine experience, that is Jeevanmukti.

151. Be content with what you have at a given time,
     Don't worry about the unattained and its missed
        result,
     Don't you worry about what you want to achieve.

152. Mistakes made will show you the right path,
     It will give you helping hand for what to be done,
     Veteran support and serious advice will guide you.

153. Humanitarianism is a bridge to socialness,
      Helping others you must be able to do well,
      Good culture strengthens the sense of socialness.

154. Energy, courage and perseverance jell with
          endurance,
      With competence we can achieve discretion and
          excellence,
      Our cognition will shun differences and foster
          socialness.

155. Thought gives the needed strength to the work plan,
      Relaxed initiation makes functioning easy and cosy,
      All is possible with peace of mind, contentement
          and faith.

156. Don't forget that for every action there will be a
          reaction,
      Make sure you run every action in well thought out
          direction,
      The crop would be as good as the seed and field
          turn out to be.

157. Equality, reciprocity should be our rudder,
      Focussed attention is integral to our efficiency,
      Patience and meditation lend support to our
          knowledge.

158. Calmness and detachment illuminate our minds,
      Only then can can we enlighten others' minds,
      All of these are contributors to our self-esteem.

159.	Good thinking leads to good speech,
	Compassion leads to good vision,
	Good vision, good words add to excellence.

160.	The bliss of salvation is within ourselves,
	Detachment will be the source of good health,
	Benevolence enlivens our mind and spirit.

161.	Give all creatures help and affection,
	Good beliefs strengthen our demeanour,
	Steps are here to Jeevanmukti, not somewhere else.

162.	Discernment requires a review of our studies,
	It is a test of attention and breadth of our study,
	With discernment develops and shines our
		discretion.

163.	Education is not for arguments and disceptations,
	Education is learning, for discussion and
		enlightenment,
	Religious education is to realize Him,not for blind
		acceptance.

164.	The idol is only a reflection of the conception of a
		Deity,
	Our goal is reinforcing a sense of divinity with a
		visual form,
	Truth and effort are instrumental in realising
		Divinity.

Vennelakanti Prakasam

165. Start with cleanliness and continue with industry,
Know that what is not harvested is not cooked,
With ethics righteousness, without ethics decay.

166. Religion should strengthen and ensure humanism,
Loathing is mindless work and it is irreligious,
Hurting and insulting others in the name of religion
is blasphemy.

167. Think beyond your clans and identify humanity,
Behave beyond your sect and tread the ethical path,
Work for us should be for the good of all.

168. Agape, kindness, help all are one,
Agape is the true demonstration of life,
Cuisine and apparel differences are of no value.

169. Character and action are important to build relations,
Friendship is the real bondage for spousality,
Sweet cohabitation is heavenly experience.

170. If the Supreme is one so is the Conscieousness in
all of us,
All humans are one and the differences are only in
appearences,
All ornaments have the same metal, don't forget.

171. Religiosity is for the realization of the self and the
Superself,
Studying other paths will free us from delusion,
Ridicule and slander without awareness is sinful,

172. Merge personal nature with societal nature,
Identify the life value of all beings,
Identify the divine presence in all human beings.

173. Education for all, respect for all and compassion for
all,
Tolerence for differences and respect for evolved
souls,
Psychological elevation is more valuable than social
conversion.

174. Avoid the anguish of argumentation and
discontentment,
Prefer awareness and enlightenment to achieve
success,
Achieve coordination and amity among your
companions.

175. Do not attribute diversity to the Supreme,
Understand the oneness of Jivatma and Paramatma,
If the mind is pious, God can be realized.

176. Practise Unity at all times with all people,
Achieve Equality all the time among all the groups,
Share Love all the time without any inhibition.

177. Wish for a vital village and love-filled world,
Every work should get proper value and right
reward,
Let's not forget all work is divinely inspired.

178. Patience, equanimity, love and forgiveness are the
          path,
      With or without Name or Form do not ignore
          Effulgence,
      Identify that unifying effulgence in all the beings.

179. Don't trouble others, especially the weaker ones,
      The ants can torment even the elephant sometimes,
      A big snake also may die at the hands of ants.

180. See mother's love in the teacher,
      See father's guidance in the teacher,
      Visualise Divinity in the teacher.

181. Excess should be axed all the time,
      Moderation should be maintained all the time,
      In food, finance and infatuation maintain
          moderation.

182. Shut the gates on lust and hate,
      Your quest should rest with dutifulness.
      Transcend the dualities to achieve peace and
          happiness.

183. Set your limits according to your aptitude,
      Arrange your equipment treasures as needed,
      Customize the flavours depending on the opportunity.

184. Place goodness in your mind along with prayer,
      Increase the good and share it with others,
      There can be no other Divine feeling than that.

185. Your language is your ornament, think and speak,
     Know that the word needs mind as source,
     There should be no difference between word and
          action.

186. The tree not giving shade, the rich not giving help
          are wasteful,
     The bridge that cannot stand and the ridge that
          cannot quench are waste,
     Affluance which is of no use is harmful, learn to
          share.

187. Avoid the weeds and lillys will abound,
     Stay away from followers who do not wish you well,
     Make good friends and help the present group.

188. Dovetail your talent with that of others,
     Dovetail your toil with that of others,
     Dovetail your goodwill and achieve Redwood
          mindset.

189. No crop means no cooking and no flour for food,
     Without work no wellbeing, so reward the worker,
     The flowering family blossoms, remember the
          creator.

190. Don't ignore the dirt, it can flirt with your eyes,
     Observe all creation, identify appropriate function,
     Everything that helps in your work deserves your
          appreciation.

                                      Vennelakanti Prakasam

191. Be cool in anger and let calm words come out
        soothing,
      Words have value, a jewel doesn't have, blabber
        may result in rancour,
      Weigh your words and use carefully, no harshness
        only sweetness.

192. Listen, observe, think,and then speak
      Don't give a word if you can't fulfil, you will lose
        faith,
      Your value is in your words, not in the jewels.

193. Shun empty words, don't blindly accept all
        sermonings,
      Words that can become actions and words that can
        do good,
      Words filled with meaning will become your
        comrades.

194. Without perception there can be no
        comprehension,
      Without comprehension there should be no
        declaration,
      No silly arguements and no unfullfillable promises.

195. No procrastination, no salivation, only fulfilment is
        good,
      With knowledge achieve equality and equanimity,
      Help as many as you can, taking it as an act of
        devotion.

196. Righteousness and truthfulness are true spiritual
        exercises,
      The feeling of Equality is the real accomplishment
        of brotherhood,
      Staying away from evil is the base virtue of existence.

197. It is a sin to attribute bias to Divinity,
      It is a sin to think flattery is important for Divinity,
      It is a sin to say worship is unavoidable for Divinity.

198. Suppress your ego and crush your pride,
      Abandon fury and hedonism totally,
      Keep away greed and unbridled desires.

199. The wisdom of the one transcending dualities is
        great,
      Worship of the feet of those overcoming dualities is
        great,
      Following the path of those transcenders is feasible.

200. Without rain no agriculture and famine is the result,
      Without comprehension no knowledge, prejudice is
        the result,
      Know that the root cause of all difficulties is
        ignorance.

201. Driving away from desires, smart man moves to
        detachment,
      With wisdom will guide others and do them good,
      Recognize the superiority of the knower and listen
        to his words.

  Vennelakanti Prakasam

202.　The virtue of 'think - speak -act alikers' is Divinity,
　　　Phasing out malevolence, fury, envy and hatred
　　　　　results in Divinity,
　　　Let that virtue shine with you till your eternity.

203.　The altruist's benevolence is virtuous affluence,
　　　Forgiving the wrongdoer and helping the do gooder
　　　　　is virtuous affluence,
　　　Treating all as one and providing assistance is
　　　　　virtuous affluence.

204.　Love should be there all over the householder's
　　　　　house,
　　　And all kinds of charities should be in operation,
　　　The same love and charity will benefit the
　　　　　householder.

205　A helpful householder is better than all abandoning
　　　　　ascetic,
　　　The householder feeding others and then himself is
　　　　　better than an ascetic,
　　　There is nothing better than marriage, harmony
　　　　　and hospitality.

206.　Home value, cooking vigilance, crop balance,
　　　There is no angel other than the well informed and
　　　　　calm minded spouse,
　　　A Virtuous, dutiful and fearless husband is the
　　　　　guardian angel.

207. Parental behavior influences the child's behaviour.
Their Redwood mindset ensures the couple's
affectionate bond,
Charitable giving should be everyone's intention for
family honour.

208. Those who do not love cannot be aligned,
For the loving ones all are theirs, no one is the other,
Love is the instrument for equality, excellence and
governance.

209. Love and righteousness of the self is the base for all
life,
Loving friendship is the helm of marriage,
Such a sweet partnership is indeed Heaven.

210. Love takes us on the straight path, avoid the wrong
path,
Loveless person's mind dries and his life is a
deserted path,
Love is water, love is oxygen, love is the digestive fire.

211. There is no meritorious deed beyond hospitality,
Hospitality filled with love is greater than all the
sacrifices,
A householder who knows the value of hospitality
is a blessed soul.

212. Crops are plentiful for the well hosting householder,
At the end the hands will dry for the non-hosting one,
Giving enriches and there will be plentiful returns.

213. The non-giving haves will end up in penury,
The weak sharer will be blessed with food, clothing
and shelter,
The householder satisfied in all aspects is a Divine
being.

214. Word's value is factualism and gentleness is the
shine of the word,
A word with a smile keeps distance from disputation,
With smilng gentleness a word gets unlimited
friendship.

215. Gentle conversation and truthful words lead to
sinlessness,
The mention of doing good to others may kindle in
us kindness,
Knowing the good of sweetness, why the sin of
harshness?

216. Good-hearted selfless service is commendable,
Don't forget the good you got, show gratitude,
The ungratefulness is most miserable of all sins.

217. Ignore the wound, forgive the doer,
Remembering even the slightest help, appreciate
the doer,
Helping is the main fundamental of humanity.

218. The good done will influence generations,
Forget the bad that happened and intend good,
Contentment to the mind and crown to your glory.

219. Goodness shines, the harshness of greed sinks,
A word without a twist and a prick for someone's
good
Will be of a great help, wherever and whenever.

220. Practice emollience, equality and equanimity,
Result will be popularity, prosperity and prowess,
Progress, piety, pabulum will be the fragrance.

221. There is no penance beyond temperance,
Controlled speech will lead to effective speech,
Restrain the rage and poise will adorn you.

222. Virtuous conduct is worthier than luxurious life,
For anyone propriety is the greatest ornament,
The knower does not forget the value of propriety
and virtue.

223. Lusting others is the first step to fall,
Mating with non-mates is the destructive last step,
Sticking to one's scope will enhance their virtuescape.

224. Show patience like the Earth and tolerate the wrong
doer,
A nonhost is a have-not and a forbearer is a strong
person,
Skill will lead you forward, patience coming along.

225. Ignore the harm and do not harm the harmer,
Fix the strong hooligan with patience,
Wish everyone well, shunning envy and jealousy.

226. The nonwealth of the good man is better than the
        wealth of the envious,
      Don't you ever eye the wealth of the known have.
      Injustice and iniquity are not for you and don't seek
        momentary pleasure.

227. Virtuous feeling is greater than enjoyment,
      Your wealth of virtue is more valuable than the
        wealth of others,
      Self-earned is the right standard from all angles.

228. What you cannot say before, don't you ever say
        behind,
      Backbiting is worse than front cheating,
      Rear venom is more dangerous than snake venom.

229. Don't praise if you don't like, but don't despise even
        if you are angry,
      Sort out the differences with words and friendship
        will result,
      Strengthen the good that is seen in others and
        better will be the results.

230. Negative words about the absentee will lose the
        faith of the presentee,
      Know that vanity is the antidote to glory,
      Wrong words are reproachful even if they are
        sweetened.

231. The virtuous wise will not talk erroneous nonsense,
      Say things related to you and the listeners,
      Use eloquent speech which harms no one.

232. The sin-fearers do not look at the curve of inequity,
      What should not happen to you should not happen
          to others,
      Enemy may cool down, but sin will have serious
          concesequences.

233. Don't seek any return for the good you have done,
      What we have is for the subsistence and happiness
          of others,
      Our energy if well utilised achieves the
          emancipation of life.

234. Invaluable support comes forth when the existing
          wealth is well shared,
      Good man's money is equal to a tree that settles
          your health,
      The knower of the value of duty chooses to share
          even in difficult times.

235. Giving to the have-not is best, Sattvic,
      Giving to the returning is medium, Rajasic,
      Giving for selfish wrong purpose is the worst,
          Tamasic.

236. Satisfy the hunger of the needy by dipping it in the
        lake of your wealth,
    Burn down the have-not's difficulties in your sacred
        fire of charity,
    There will never be a real shortage of wealth for the
        one who shares.

237. The miserly saviour of wealth is more wreched than
        a beggar,
    The eradicater of others' poverty is better than the
        one who seeks Heaven,
    Get fame with your deeds and inspire your children.

238. The wealth of kindness is better than the wealth of
        money any day,
    The worker who helps is better than the have who
        does not give,
    Cultivate the nectar of love plants in the heart of
        compassion.

239. Kindness richness is better than the wealth
        richness,
    One day the one who has no money will get money,
    The merciless without change of heart is doomed.

240. How come you take another life for your life,
    For self-defence if essential it is okay,
    Think whether you should do it for taste and
        appetite.

241. Saving an animal is better than pouring butter oil in
        Homam,
     It's not even worth hurting a fellow human being,
     It is a divine act trying to save the living beings.

242. It is penance enduring one's suffering without
        hurting others,
     It is penance striving for abstinence and temperance,
     It is nonpenance adopting fraudulent restraint
        measures.

243. Fructification cannot be achieved by nonpenance,
     Pretending fraudulent holiness will result in serious
        remorse,
     The virus of wrong will follow you but the glow of
        right will flow with you.

244. Don't you ever cheat if you wish to avoid notoriety,
     Wrong idea itself is sinful, don't try for smart
        wickedness,
     Fraudulent wealth will not stay,not even a bit of it.

245. Do not abandon the righteousness shown by higher
        reality,
     Speak out the truth resultant of total awareness,
     Analyze properly without ignoring material reality.

246 Righteous truth is greater than charity and penance,
     Water purifies the body and truth purifies mind,
     Spiritual progress is caused by altruistic thoughts
        and actions.

247. Tie up the anger that hurts and wounds,
       Anger like weeds will damage us, pull it out,
       The smiling face and pleasant mind should not be
          disturbed.

248. Haven't you heard that anger is our enemy,
       Health will be damaged and relations will be
          disturbed,
       Think, ponder and calm your mind.

249. Surrendering to anger is like accepting death,
       Conquering anger is defeating death,
       With serenity you achieve progress, prestige,
          prosperity.

250. The impeccable does not face envy,
       The impeccable does not bother others,
       The Impeccable will help even the harmers.

251. It is better not to cause loss of life than not to be far
          from truth,
       The fear of death doesn't touch if you don't cause
          death,
       Set right the offender's path and save his life.

252. There is no harm in giving up an item of pleasure,
       Avoid the use of addictive objects and seek only
          calm energy,
       Forsake excess, increase detachment and enhance
          sharing.

253. Lower 'I'ness and 'My'ness, smash the rods of
          desire,
      Destroy the monsters of suspicion and distrust,
      Demolish ignorance,be alert and realize awareness.

254. Get rid of desire, anger and aimlessness,
          wickedness will perish,
      The fear of the cycle of birth and death will be
          eliminated,
      The basis of all is truth, love, and piety that lead us
          to Divinity.

255. Desire can contaminate any kind of mind,
      If it is set aside the route is set to immortality,
      The route of 'think- speak- and -act alike' leads to
          emancipation.

256. With the planetary picture is fixed the psychosoma,
      The path to goodness is paved by hard work,
      Knowledge and Wealth accrue and Calmness is
          important.

257. Fearlessness is valuable but caution should not be
          forsaken,
      Charity is very valuable but one's own people need
          care too,
      Strength is very valuable but its good use is more
          important.

258. Poise with gentleness and humility with knowledge
      Charity without pride and differences without clash
      Will be assets to all administrators and employment
          creators.

259. Softness in one's own language, calmness to others'
          harshness,
      Concentration on one's own work, coolness about
          the result,
      Interest to give, not keen to take will give us
          excellent humans.

260. Letters and numbers are necessary for everyone,
      Virtuous it is sharing the light of education,
      Extensive education is the source of all knowledge.

261. Education is the unseen wealth, wisdom is
          nondiminishing fount,
      Goodness is inexhaustible wealth and learning is an
          immutable mount,
      Live we should with the help of broad thinking and
          focussed interest.

262. Being silent is ingenuity in the discussion of
          unknown subject,
      The knowledge gained from experience glows well,
      Knowledge well shared is valued more than social
          identity.

263. The greatest value of all wealth is aural education,
     Blessed are the professors who add to our aural
          wealth,
     Aural knowledge also shines well without reading
          support.

264. The fortress built by the sage is his wisdom and self
          restraint,
     To recognize and comprehend the omnipresent
          truth is real intelligence,
     The wise will not let the flaws flow and fickleness to
          set foot.

265. The wise man will speak well and enlighten
          elegantly,
     The one who walks in line with the world trends is
          a realist,
     Setting aside arrogance, liquidizing fury, detaining
          desires is exaltation.

266. Purity of goal, purity of action, purity of company,
     These purities are the right ship for life voyage,
     This pact purity is indeed founding base for all.
     [Think, Speak, Act alike = This pact]

267. Time, region, situation if well contextualised,
     It will be convenient to achieve what is intended,
     All-round strength will achieve all-round
          prosperity.

268. Advice should be contingent on the value of time
          and relationship,
      Know that aptitude decides the level of our attention,
      Education and profession need to be chosen
          accordingly.

269. Self respect, wisdom, discretion and munificence,
      These four qualities will constitute a good advisor
      Patience and skill will be assets to anyone, anytime
          and anywhere.

270. Forgetfulness erodes our lives from all angles,
      All unplanned plans are wasted efforts,
      A good idea well executed will yield right results.

271. Subtlety is a useful tool for any officer,
      A fair and quick decision builds reputation,
      Justice gives true satisfaction to one and all.

272. Death for the enemy in battle but if surrendered
          refuge,
      Punishment according to crime, change in the
          behaviour the target,
      Power should be used for welfare but not for
          suppression.

273. Crime if neglected causes turmoil in society,
      If the work is not encouraged, the treasury will thin
          out,
      Punishment,security,affection,indifference should
          be in place.

274. Glances of compassion and love are an ornament of
         action,
      Right attention for what is said is an ornament to
         the ears,
      Smile and gentle speech will become the lips.

275. The officer should know that he is responsible,
      Show the way and share the task with the subordinates,
      Provide adequate facilities as per their requirement.

276. Eyes are the tools for spy, ears are important for the
         officer,
      Memory and tact are important for all public figures,
      The real goal is to reduce the bad and increase the
         good.

277. Talent, perseverance, efficiency will bring success,
      Success, humility and gentleness bring good name,
      Good name will lengthen the support of kinsmen
         and friends.

278. Patience, practicality, perception proper,
      If these three join hands with tact and care.
      The officer will enjoy allround success.

279. Non-rhythmic song, merciless glances, an unkept
         word,
      A sword that cannot save the kin, a householder
         who cannot be a host,
      Should undergo transformation and then be
         appreciated by everyone.

280. Narcolepsy and lethargy are a threat to family
       honour,
     Work not done in time and work unfulfilled in time
       bring bad name,
     The one who cannot comprehend when told can
       become a problem.

281. It is good to be able to comprehend without being
       taught,
     Those who do not understand even when taught
       can be a problem,
     Using words as butter and helping others in need is
       better.

282. With courage and determination we can overcome
       adversity,
     The haves who do not misdemean will not sink
       while in penury,
     As if a full pot they will remain calm with contentment.

283. Everything is possible if time and tool are in hand,
     Full grip, overall security and clarity are steps to
       success,
     With appropriate skills, changes and additions are
       possible.

284. Listening to knower's worthy word is appropriate,
     The word is a fortress if clarity, truthfulness and
       fullness are in,
     With meaning weighty and style candy the word is
       binding.

285.	The teared property of others will lead to further tears,
	What is earned of one's own work will satiate fully,
	Unsteady thinking will lead to unsure stepping.

286.	The scholar who shines and smiles is highly
		admired and praised,
	The nongreedy need-fulfilling merchant is loved
		and supported,
	The graceful officer assisting in time is appreciated
		and respected.

287.	Ward off the wicked, attend to the ailing and feed
		the hungry,
	Educators should establish assiduous schools in
		new localities,
	The leaders and officials should win the
		appreciation of the people.

288.	Wealth acquired by right means will lead to
		allround happiness,
	Comprehensive knowledge will always provide
		appropriate solutions,
	Natural herbal remedies do not do any harm if well
		used.

289.	Strength, courage, discernment and memory are
		essential pillars,
	These pillars effect the security of the inside and
		also of the outside,
	Rulers and leaders can then make right decisions
		for the people.

 Vennelakanti Prakasam

290. Friendship is unfading and ever shining golden
        bond,
    Beyond selfishness, friendship is the everlasting
        relationship,
    The spousal bond, a conjugating bond, is ultimately
        the Divine bond.

291. Modesty is important to get acceptance among the
        people,
    With modesty poise will not be misunderstood,
    Modesty with education will be like fragrance to
        gold.

292. Character and conduct are more important than
        family background,
    Right conduct is the result if right path is chosen
        and treaded,
    Only enlightened truth can yield completeness of
        vision.

293. Spontaneous self esteem dispenses nice perfume if
        well nurtured,
    Self and otherness feeling will not come up if
        properly cultured,
    Treating others as one's own is the ultimate Divine
        path.

294. Giving alms as public service is welcome,
    Alms to patronize is considered inappropriate,
    We can give as much as we can, but no bad language.

295. The real fear should be about doing something bad,
The real hesitation should about fibbing,
The real adamancy should be to do good to others.

296. Ploughing is to keep the air blowing and to help in
weeding out
Sunshine and water are to energize and also
fertilizers to add on,
Above all these the attention of the farmer's keen
eye is great for the crop.

297. Slow the swing of sight so as not to swipe,
Do not let the bullets go off from the eyebrow
bows,
The honey of love in the heart is important, right!

298. The sharpness of the gaze and the sharpness of the
fruit taste,
The cool call of the alectoris and the unreachable
fragrant twig,
The heart which cools down flippancy are all very
important.

299. Alcohol intoxicates, arrogance pushes,
Fistcuff gives swelling but learning gives ideas,
Charity gives a shine to the charm of socialness.

300. Tighten the mind, think about tomorrow,
Work for society and all illusions will vanish,
Cherish the Divine in you and also among others.

301. Silence is the refuge in the discussion of the
           unknown subject,
      Wisdom is the light for the arrogance of darkness,
      Save your discretion to prevent the avoidable fall.

302. There is no antidote to foolishness and no
           atonement for ingratitude,
      Humans cannot shine without any fragrance of art,
      Where is civilization if wisdom, generosity and
           piety lack?

303. Access to education is beneficial to one and all,
      It is our responsibility to provide minimum
           facilities for all,
      Unbiased provision for education excels even
           modesty as a great quality.

304. There is no weapon beyond love, no shield beyond
           endurance,
      No enemy beyond anger, no weakness beyond
           haughtiness,
      There is no gift beyond strengthening the weak
           have-not.

305. With the knower we can get to know the things
           that matter,
      Selfishness will weaken with the company of
           help-giver,
      If all the companions are worthy why any other
           wealth at all?

306. Wise it is staying away from violence and being
          close to true wording,
      Wise it is being reasonably charitable and being
          inaccessible to greed,
      Wise it to be respectful to the elders and extend
          agape to one and all.

307. Humility, modesty and shyness are okay but not
          meekness,
      Pride, arrogance, and harshness should be shunned
          but not courage,
      Agility and tact should be there but certainly not
          deceit.

308. Do not waste things which are useful and can be
          used,
      In excitement do not use words that are unmeaning
          or hurting,
      Use your wealth appropriately, save it and do not
          sink it in mire.

309. A crop shared with those in need is valuable,
      Of what use if hidden and preyed upon by animals
          and insects,
      It must be used, must be shared,but not let be
          wasted.

                                        Vennelakanti Prakasam

310. Do not despise a fruit-bearing tree or a crop-
bearing field,
Do not neglect those who can help poor kinsmen
and friends,
Do not forget calmness in plenty and alertness
when in penury.

311. Power, fame, feasting, and helping the learned are
right,
We have to provide the have-nots with love and
sympathy,
Life flourishes on one's own nature, planetary
stature and work culture.

312. Even for the wise cruelty, envy and greed are
dangerous,
Wealth, prestige, education are dormant if the
conduct is unbecoming,
Set the goals with constant intellection and
evaluation.

313. The wicked does not look at any talent with
admiration
Self-assessment and shunning the wrong path are
of a great help,
Increase the good and reduce the bad and flourish
comfortably.

314. Excessive anger does not strengthen the bond of
        alliance,
      If good qualities dovetail like redwood roots they
        will shine,
      A strong man shuns weaknesses and always helps
        others.

315. Unassuming sharing mindset and a gleeful
        hospitality fit in,
      Showing gratitude and expressing appreciation will
        be right,
      Context sensitive but sensible toughness and
        softness fit in too.

316. The droplet evaporates on the hot plate but glows
        on the lotus leaf,
      The same drop of water will become a pearl in a
        pearl shell,
      A human being can become a scholar in
        contemplative company.

317. Well set life should sparkle with humility, gratitude
        and charity,
      Mindfulness, diligence and chosen toil bring forth
        good results,
      Selfless service and mutual aid are the epitome of
        self-realization.

318. Courtesy is plume for the noble, gentleness is
          plume for the leader,
       Calmness is plume for the educated, charity is
          plume for the haves,
       Silence is plume for the ascetic, and all these are
          plumes for the Wise.

319. Great is the dutifulness along with righteousness,
       If undeviated in poverty richness will come back,
       Equality and generosity are evershining double
          route.

320. Food alone is not enough for our survival,
       Makeup looks are not enough for our life,
       Our responsibilities to society are our real guide.

321. Don't test the society, treat it as Divine lake,
       Perform your duty responsibly well,
       If you forget social justice you will be a loner,

322. Do not forget your responsibilities and don't deny
          righteousness,
       Think of society as God's gift for your wellbeing,
       The consciousness within you awakens and
          blossoms.

323. Let go off the darkness and let the light flow in,
       Share with others the glow of your wisdom,
       Your way is to keep others safe from slipping.

324. Physical violence is truly flawed,
     Verbal violence is even more flawed,
     It is wrong to torture anyone for any purpose.

325. Offenses committed with the body are sins,
     Crimes committed with the mind are greater sins,
     Done with clear mind unavoidable doings are
         forgivable.`

326. Don't you ever swear nor should you go back on
         your word,
     Don't give a water bubble promise to a friend or foe,
     Foresight and sincerity are important to make a
         promise.

327. Doing harm to a harmer is an animal virtue,
     Doing good to the wicked is a noble virtue,
     Good to evil is always an antidotal virtue.

328. Righteousness is the law of justice,
     Never shrug off your role in socialness,
     Do not bear the burden of unbridled desire.

329. All are brothers except fathers and sons,
     All are sisters except for the mothers and wives,
     And for spouses, that friendship is Divine.

330. The mundane honour is only for the present,
     The cosmic peace and prosperity are forever,
     Reduce the present cravings, if you seek cosmic
         favour.

    Vennelakanti Prakasam

331. No flamboyance nor show off devotion while
          practising charity,
      Your compliance is more valuable than the
          recognition of others,
      Thispact purity will ensure your allround
          development.

332. With the passage of time money melts off,
      In the company of righteous weighty ideas grow,
      Not right it is to wish someone ill, do good to
          others with love.

333. Reflect in your eyes compassion, light and love,
      Light will come in as an antidote to darkness,
      With harshness nothing can be accomplished.

334. Realize your flaws and correct them first,
      Only then can you correct and lead others,
      Worry not about things not with you, but share
          what you have.

335. We do get back what we willingly give,
      Don't deviate and don't deceive others,
      Try to share what is sharable and usable.

336. Choose the right path even if it is narrow,
      The destination reached will please you,
      The vast evil path will plunge you into sorrow.

337. Stay away from those who mislead,
      Move forward even if it is difficult path,
      A tough but unselfish walk gets us to the shore.

338. Don't be deceived by empty words, the weight of
          truth has value,
     The believable path will lead you to the destination
          you seek,
     Believe in trustworthy deeds but never in fible-fables.

339. Passion is not enough, experience should accompany,
     Need should be accompanied by right opportunity,
     Passion, experience, need and opportunity are the
          keys to success.

340. Doctor's expertise promotes patient's relief.
     The Divine path ensures sinner's expiation,
     Follow the precepts and practices of the Divine
          beings.

341. It is not improper to hoodwink the beastly,
     It is not inappropriate to threaten those who cheat,
     For the righteous choose only the right conduct.

342. The internal toughness and external softness jell
          well,
     Internal deceipt and external sweetness constitue
          evil,
     It is bad to want to do bad to good out of envy.

343. Take precautions for the corporeal safety.
     Do not be foolhardy and don't be undernourished,
     Hygiene is important, follow the doctor's advice.

344. Elevate yourself in the spiritual excercise,
Negate the negativity and adopt positivity,
Head for things that make everyone happy.

345. Honour the righteous and respect the pious ascetics,
Respect the learned and recognise the higher ups,
Treat the unschooled natural sages as worthy beings.

346. Our words fix our status, whatever be the title,
The disrorted will be the losers, whatever be their
education,
Right wording is the bidding to avoid insults and
blames.

347 Let the seeds of knowledge germinate and grow well,
Recognition and respect do not run to you, they
walk,
Buds take time to blossom and flowers take time to
fruition.

348. Remove the weeds of distraction within the realm
of knowledge,
Include details of different topics in your intellection,
Study what is heard, what is remembered and what
is recorded.

349. Harshness and cruelty to the weak bring disgrace,
Being compassionate towards the weak brings glory.
Removing the poverty of the poor is indeed Divine
service.

350. Perfection in faith, diligence in action,
     Will bring strength to us and good will be the result,
     If modesty is with us, other's help will come to us.

351. What you eat does not really defile you,
     Your actions that harm others will defile you,
     Kep your ideation, your verbalisation and your
          praxis undefiled.

352. Devotion and power in words should emanate from
          your thinking
     Piety in actions should also emanate from your
          ideas,
     All beautiful things emerge from the serenity of
          your thinking.

353. Waive off the loans from ones who cannot give,
     As regards your dues, proffer to give on time,
     Change your lifestyle to concur your wherewithal.

354. The foundation for a marital bond must be solid,
     Don't you ever seek release, never at all,
     Couples are bound to strengthen social progress.

355. Acquire sufficient wealth unto yourself,
     Share your wealth with others as per your budget,
     The undue weight of wealth afflicts a variety of people.

356. Wishing good of others is true prayer,
     Giving a helping hand to others is the real worship,
     Seeing the Divine in all is real salvation.

                                    Vennelakanti Prakasam

357. Safe it is to be distant from what is not yours,
      Smartness it is protecting what is yours gently,
      Fairness it is to distribute evenly to all the kinsmen.

358. Attraction, affection, confidence, preference will be
          excelled by agape,
      Surreder to the Supreme Being with fully
          blossomed agape,
      Swim with any stream and across any sea with the
          Primordial Love.

359. Self-praise creates a variety of pitfalls,
      Blasphemy is dangerous in all its forms.
      Delightful indeed it is modest self-appreciation and
          exaltation.

360. Nonpatronising genuine brotherliness is fair,
      No one believes the unrelishable flattery,
      Irrelevant criticism is not welcome, even if not
          untrue.

361. Prayer is important, not the gold in the temple,
      Faith, mercy, and justice are supremely important,
      Your word and your hospitality are important but
          not showing off.

362. Be alert and ready all the time to receive,
      Who knows when the blessings pour in or shower
          on,
      Shun arrogance and avoid intoxication, blessed you
          will be.

363. What is useful for long and for many is the right
         path,
    What is useful for the timebeing is subsistence,
    The thing that works only for some depreciates.

364. Pay close attention to what you are doing,
    Carelessness does all sorts of damage,
    Do not neglect what is needed, result will be
         shortage,

365. Violence leads to violence and many will suffer,
    Be peaceful, be just and the result will be right,
    Try to cool down violence and,if not possible,
         retaliate.

366. Right path, selfless tread will make the goal upright,
    Ignore flamboyant godmen who actually mislead,
    Trust the people who are calm and who guide
         correctly.

367. Keep away from the ones who go astray,
    Listen to the ones who can explain different paths,
    Social welfare and progress is of paramount
         importance.

368. Pay due attention at the timing of sowing,
    All kinds of profit will flow out at the time of
         harvest
    If you do not sow, you cannot reap at all.

Vennelakanti Prakasam

369. Trust yields fruit, peace will prevail,
      Understand that your well-being is in others'
          well-being,
      Intense empathy towards society will achieve
          emancipation.

370. Keep the mind clear and pure in all matters,
      Deformity and depravity will not touch you ever,
      Only help will be ensured for you and no harm.

371. Tradition and ritual are for the good of people,
      What is not good to people has no traditional
          value,
      Humans and other living beings should live well,
          right?

372. All prayers should strengthen your hand,
      What weakens you is certainly not a prayer,
      Become selective and moderate consumer of ideas
          that help.

373. Renunciation is good but not derilection of duty,
      Sacrifice is good but the thispact should not suffer,
      You have to be upright and also right to other
          friends.

374. Do not enjoy at the expense of others,
      Strive for satisfaction, seek others' help,
      Reward well for the assistance received.

375. Ponder over and accept the word of the saints,
     Implement only what is practicable and helpful,
     Only after your experience guide others along the
          right path.

376. Don't surrender to undue greed, give value to
          contentment,
     Save what you have and share it reasonably with
          others,
     The others will help you whenver you need
          something.

377. Feed the hungry with what you have right away,
     Clothe the naked with what you can spare right
          away,
     Helping others in need is much greater than
          sermonising,

378. Those in danger must be rescued immediately,
     Do not highlight your problems to escape,
     Know that saving others in time is a Divine act.

379. False swearing will lead to serious backlash,
     Forgiving and showing the right path will benefit,
     It is Divine helping even harmer when you can.

380. Think logically, articulate clearly, there will be no
         problems,
      Dexterity while planning and diligence in doing will
         be in order,
      Work will be completed, there will no blaming and
         fruition will be ensured.

381. The ones who help you while in need are yours
         indeed,
      Your people keeping distance are outsiders anyway,
      Reciprocity is the base for this life you should know.

382. We tell others to transcend the dualities,
      The mind does not listen, the heart does not
         cooperate.
      Meditation only can make the mind listen and
         operate.

383. Without social justice higher activity gets derailed,
      Without economic justice there can be no real
         progress in the society,
      Without cultural justice there can be no worthwhile
         society.

384. Freedom of speech is not for lavish talk,
      Smart talk is not at all misrepresentation,
      Oratory is not languaging light a thundering cloud.

385. All that is natural and for all is sattvic love,
      What we show for name and returns is rajasic love,
      Pretending love with selfish end is tamasic love.

386. Demonstrate efficiency while doing,
Show sweetness while speaking,
Shower cool grace while looking.

387. You don't need auspicious time to do good to others,
Believe that a good mindset is precious and pure,
Be noble, be altruistic and be dovetailed like
redwood.

388. No bragging only gentleness, growth is certain,
Do not violate norms except for the welfare of others,
Except in self-defence do not break the law.

389. The Divine abode is your wonderful heart,
Wake up and witness that world in all the beimgs,
Encourage the helpful and find a way to change the
harmful.

390. Don't you think you are responsible for success or
failure,
Your value is in finishing with diligence what you
have started,
Leave the fruit to the circumstances and
supervention.

391. While praying or worshipping do it with
concentration,
Do not hold a negative attitude towards anyone,
Only positive attitude with full attention can yield
good results.

392. Do not succumb to mischief and crave not for petty
         things,
      Don't run away from responsibilities, loss will be
         the result,
      Doing your duty is you ladder and the goal is
         liberation.

393. Come out of darkness and see the light,
      Ignore the profit part and show interest in work,
      Clarity of goal, interest and diligence will do wonders.

394. Words alone are not enough to achieve a goal,
      The acts should be skilful and methodical,
      Lending helping hand to many is the real act.

395. It is necessary to forgive the erring others,
      For this there should be love for everyone,
      If mind is pious love will sprout everywhere.

396. Faith drives us forward very coolly,
      Don't ridicule others, fakeness will not sell,
      Truth and firmness will do all the pushing job.

397. If you sow neem, neem will be the fruit,
      Service to parents will bear the right fruit,
      Great indeed is what we do to orphans and have-nots.

398. Harassing, torturing and killing are forbidden
      Cleanliness outside, piety inside will be your shield,
      Achieve your neighbours' reconciliation, right step
         to salvation.

399. Purity of mind is the basic formatting,
What matters is the truth of the words,
Piety in your work is the path to the other world,

400. Work or charity beyond one's calibre is unwelcome,
Unpretentious and egalitarian you ought to be,
The society will recognize and help you in many ways.

401. Support unsupported women and the elderly,
Let them move forward according to their mind,
However goodwill and detachment are helpful.

402. Do not seduce the minds of others in the name of
religion,
Do not intimidate others in the name of religion,
It is best to ignore mistakes and support them with
words of love.

403. God's existence assures impartialality and due
recognition,
God is beyond flattery and expansion of his influence,
Admission to Hell or Heaven is not identity-based
but on thispact purity.

404. Don't seek publicity when you hurt and help,
Charity and compassion should be like twins,
Then recognition will come without any publicity.

405. With awareness we become enlightened,
It is wisdom helping others, setting aside profit,
Waiving a loan is also a sign of wisdom.

 Vennelakanti Prakasam

406. Righteousness and virtuous living will emancipate
       us,
     Do not argue about things you are not conversant
       with,
     Do not deviate from what is known for selfishness.

407. There can be no better mindset than honesty,
     Don't you ever support untruth or distrust,
     Do not deceive the ones who trust you and others.

408. The pigeon has to fly to enjoy the ascent,
     Give with love and joy while giving to others,
     The correct path provides the easy way to move
       forward.

409. The wicked will perforce be finally humiliated,
     The good will certainly reap right results,
     Everyone appreciates what is given in the
       appropriate context.

410. Atone for all the sins that were committed,
       knowingly or unknowingly,
     It is essential to practise goodness as part of
       thispact purity,
     Do not ignore the awareness which is the base of
       all.

411. Seek and achieve what is deserving,
     Cultivate only the convenient crops,
     Enjoy what will be right from all angles.

412. Social compliance is the best of all adornments,
Prayer is Divine but not flamboyance,
Do not forget time and context while choosing attire.

413. Pride is primary disturber of our mental purity,
Greed burrows into our personality building,
Atonement improves us from all angles.

414. The weak, the sick, the destitute deserve forgiveness,
The Divine humans deem it right to help them,
Mercy will not be shown on the greedy and arrogant.

415. A good guide is one who neither wrongs nor counts
    your wrongs,
He will be worth the blessings of many a Divine
    human,
Move ahead with patience, skill and perseverance.

416. Impartial justice and generosity are signs of Divinity
Hidden crimes and niggardness are most
    unwelcome,
The humble, the helpful and the grateful are blessed
    by Divinity.

417. Know that unacceptable combinations are
    precarious,
Unhealthy pleasures will finally cause grief,
Enjoy all the comforts and pleasures within
    bounds.

418. The eye on the orphan's property is eye on the
         lightning,
      Care for him,help him and plan to make him a have,
      Do not acquire power and authority through secret
         means.

419. Gentleness and enjoyment of appropriate pleasures
         will be right,
      It is better to undertake known virtuous activities,
      Then right here you will have heavenly pleasures.

420. Stay away from those who are a bit too secretive,
      Showing off may bring you down, restraint is helpful,
      Forgiveness will glow as love of living beings.

421. The core of your mind is what actually matters,
      Fradulence will not work and it will cause your fall,
      Let your words be your feet and truth your tongue,
         and world smiles.

422. Lenience in looks, tact in talk and grace in gait,
      With all these your heart will be filled with
         ambrosia of love,
      No faultfinding, only praising the positive, you will
         receive encomiums.

423. The right path is readily available to those who trust,
      All success is for those who lend support to others,
      Blessed one wll guide onto the right path the frauds
         and haters.

424. The one who does good without asking for fruit is a
      sattvic,
    The one who does good seeking result is rajasic,
    The one who does good with fraudulent mind
      tamasic.

425. Words are seeds, fruit giving trees are our action,
    The words of the righteous are the steps necessary
      for salvation,
    No hypocrisy, Real Faith and Community Service
      are the best.

426. Give value to the wealth before your eyes,
    The pure wealth of the mind is priceless,
    All that is needed for anyone is virtuous thispact.

427. Reform yourself first before you think of others,
    Then set out to put others on the right path,
    All reforms are for the protection of fellow beings.

428. Do listen to your parents and be upright,
    Serve your parents and be fully satisfied,
    Stand up as an ideal for your children and their
      children.

429. Handling unknown things create problems,
    Know that gentleness will bring glow to your
      education,
    Know the limits of education and no one is perfect,
      right?

     Vennelakanti Prakasam

430. Adequate wages should pass on to workers
          immediately,
      Pay a little more,smile a bit and shun labour theft,
      A thief cannot escape punishment with the fake
          chanting.

431. Don't misuse your intelligence, put it to right use,
      Strength should be used to protect others but not
          to cause harm,
      Be righteous while earning money and while
          spending money.

432. Encourage the doer of good, it will be all gain,
      Drag the evil ally back to the right path,
      Forgive the mistakes of others, your mistakes will
          be forgiven.

433. Admire one and all, differentiation is useless,
      Do the work diligently, distraction is useless,
      Seek duty and be patient about the results.

434. Bad will result if you try to enjoy the unspeakable,
      Blame not others for your wrongdoing, no one will
          buy it,
      Understand, analyze, and correct your shortcomings.

435. Relying on others totally is neither wise nor
          appropriate,
      Self-sufficiency is best in all ways and at all times,
      Creating self-sufficiency for others is of paramount
          value.

436. Ego will dry you up beyond rehydration,
      There is nothing to gain from unnecessary
          compliments,
      Enough recognition and respect is enough, be
          gentle.

437. Forgiveness eradicates affliction and both are
          blessed,
      Soft and sweet talk reinforces compatibility of
          people,
      Your actions shadow you, good deeds are par
          excellence.

438. Wisdom is for prosperity, strength for sustenance,
          devotion for salvation,
      For the glow of the mundane world good deeds are
          must,
      Whatever you can do for other's welfare is a good
          deed.

439. Support the meek and needy and stand by them,
      Ignore the greedy people and give up wasteful
          spending,
      Focus on the task in hand and achieve the result.

440. Generosity is the real power you have,
      Forgiveness is the extra power you have,
      Pay attention to peace and fellow feeling.

441. Determination is required in all matters,
      Whether about the goal or about the strategic path,
      Faith, peace and goodwill are your tools.

442. No swording with wrong intention and for wrong
         purposes,
      Your ideas and words shouldn't be unshattered
         knives of prejudices,
      Demonstrate skill with love and discipline for
         others' welfare.

443. You are the right spouse if there is love in your words
      You are the right spouse if there is verve in your
         nerve,
      You are the right spouse if you are a man in need
         and deed.

444. You are the right spouse if you have sweetness in
         your words,
      You are the right spouse if there is warmth in your
         cuddling,
      You are the right spouse if you are with him all the
         time.

445. If you don't want famine the crops should get water
         and manure,
      To be in good repute you should be a man of word
         well kept,
      Education needs gentleness to have a glowing
         appeal.

446. The drizzle should not irritate if you want ponds to
         be filled
      Don't look down on grains if you want the
         grainhouse to be filled
      Don't belittle prayers if you want others to be
         positive and helpful.

447. As the flour, so is the bread; as the savings, so is the
         having,
      As the calves, so is running; as the sight, so is the
         proximity,
      It will be all good if you see the limits and run
         forward smartly.

448. Affection for the mind, courage for the heart,
      Stability for walking, and persevarence for work,
      Depth in writing are the real shining jewellery.

449. The earthly dust teaches us gentleness,
      The planetary power teaches us nobility,
      The spirit in us will wake up the divinity in us.

450. Calmness and endurance are twins,
      Everything is possible with their support,
      Greed, ego and infatuation are dangerous trins.

451. Earthly link and pressure are of no use,
      Selfless service to society is of immense value,
      The route to emancipation is from service unto
         others.

452. Introversion is never a slippery slope,
      Extroversion is for duty services only,
      Only then will one be oriented to divinity,
          transcending dualities.

453. The value of repentance is righteous conduct,
      A change in mental instinct will ensure spiritual
          freedom,
      Practice and meditation are more important than
          rituals.

454. Satisfaction, selflessness and truth are your tristand,
      That will be your pedestial of worship and prayer,
      Others will tread your path inspired by your conduct.

455. Your experience leads to fresh understanding,
      Clarity improves and the vision angle improves,
      The Cicerone will show you the light and the Saints
          will bless you.

456. In mentor's light the problems can be scraped and
          sifted,
      Simplicity in thought and gentleness in looks
          strengthen devotion,
      The wealth of virtuous will not let pomposity come
          in.

457. Imagine all to be in you, the divinity gets formed,
      Desires and worries keep healthy distance from you,
      Doubts will vanish and the triad of TAB will flourish.
      [*TAB; Truth, Awareness and Bliss]

458. Your effort is to give effect to sympathy,
     Your anxiety,rather eagerness, is for the welfare of
          all,
     All your exuberance is for the peace and prosperity
          of others.

459. The same spirit of Awareness we have there in dog
          and pig,
     Recognize the Awareness in every being and
          respect it,
     All should play a role in the strengthening of their
          group.

460. Bondage and asceticism do not at all jell,
     The absence of attachment is a symbol of true
          righteousness,
     The feeling of bigness will melt, being cool and
          calm is fine.

461. Giving generosity is a good thing, whenever possible,
     Miserliness and greed do indeed reflect meanness,
     The needed frugality is welcome from all angles.

462. Desire perseverance, work hard and stability will
          set it in,
     Evaluate the surroundings from your own perspective,
     Reality does not come from others' perspective.

463. Enmity for profit is totally inappropriately wrong,
     Fraud for profit is indeed punishably wrong,
     Breaking a promise for profit is unacceptably wrong.

464. Recognize the consciousness that is in all of us,
Awaken the consciousness within you,
You will get Divine knowledge very fast.

465. Ignore caste, religion, language and region,
Character, attention and skill are the jewels of a
person,
Uniqueness is in being dovetailed with others for
general good.

466. Your own nature, the surrounding culture will show
you the path,
The planetary effects will also be there with your
inclination,
However, with your effort you can outreach new
heights.

467. Blasphemy no, insulting others no,
Mistakes like that will bite you back,
Pat on other's back without any false complex.

468. Do not give in to unfounded fears,
Continue to believe in the Divine gurus,
The feeling of Divinity is the fruit of love and piety.

469. Believe and realize the spirit of Awareness in you,
Admiration and steadfastness in you will be
stronger,
Awareness travels with you and you will reap your
harvest.

470. What you eat, where you eat and when you eat do
       not really matter,
     What you think, what you say and what you do
       really matter,
     Your thoughts will lead you to positive state or
       negative state.

471. Share what you have with others and with the
       Supreme Being,
     Denying it to others may end up as not gaining for
       youself,
     You will get back only if you give what is to be given.

472. Your body is the temple of Divine consciousness,
     Yield place to positivity, shun off negativity which
       IS risky,
     Understand what you read and try to implement
       what you profess.

473. Melt off desires and seek knowledge of Awareness,
     Forsake hatred, seek the realm of peace and love,
     Drive away ignorance and become a path-showing
       knower.

474. Sift well who has come to learn and what has to be
       learnt,
     Let the useless material be dumped and thrown off,
     Wrap up meaningful seeds of knowledge to help
       the learner.

                                    Vennelakanti Prakasam

475. The icons and idols are a reflection of the Divine,
      That concept can lead us to the desired destination,
      It is our duty to follow what we believe to be true.

476. Turn the feeling of enmity into an alliance with love,
      Strengthen the mind with the words of the teacher,
      Clear your doubts,grasp the reality and develop
          dutifulness.

477. Start early,be on the track and go forward briskly,
      Don't stop if tired, just relax and move forward,
      The one who achieves even a part is a winner.

478. You know your goal and your skill is yours,
      You know your efficiency and your patience is yours,
      Why bother about others' comments, your progress
          is yours.

479. That person's commitment is worth more than who
          he is,
      Likewise reforming the offender is important, not
          punishment,
      More valuable than anxiety is focused clarity of the
          goal.

480. Focus on etiquette and treat the welfare of others as
          of great importance,
      And as a quick reward we will get the cooperation
          of others,
      Comprehension, cognition and cognizence will be
          the end result.

481. When you seek to fullfill the needs of others with
        love,
     Move forward without hesitation, even if with a
        slight loss,
     Don't seek gratitude and return gifts to match your
        deeds.

482. Focus on what you can and have to give others,
     Hunger and anger are bad for everyone in every way,
     Achieve transformation in others with gentleness
        and grace.

483. What if a dog, what if a pig, and what if a crow all
        are same beings,
     Think all are like you and are yours, then you are a
        Divine soul,
     Spread the feelings of coolness and completeness
        with grace.

484. Inward beauty is more important than outward
        shine,
     Elegant it is if gentleness goes hand in hand with
        softness,
     Confidence, diligence and patience are the real
        cream of life.

485. Know that the one above is your personal truth,
     The Cicerone is the above one's factual truth,
     Demonstrate in your actions the words of your
        mentor.

                                        Vennelakanti Prakasam

486. Recognize the Guru, believe him and join him
      Then it is easy to swim across this ocean of life,
      Truth-seeking is your need and guidance is your
          teacher's deed.

487. Achieve clarity regarding the goal before you set
          out,
      Be patient be honest and don't you ever look
          sideways,
      Achieve your goal for the welfare of your spiralling
          self.

488. The wounds on your body will disappear fast,
      Success is yours if you fasten your mental strength,
      Your faith and your courage are the real strong
          tools.

489. Take the wound as a light teaching you strategies
      Think of the obstacle as a training tool of your
          strength
      Defeat will not touch you if you don't desire wrong
          goals.

490. Overcome doubts and progress forward soberly
          and silently,
      Go with the teacher's word without sliding into any
          tempting trap,
      Be alert and achieve what you want in a pleasant
          and selfless way.

491. What you think, what you say and what you concur
   are all vows
   Be careful that the breach of oath never happens in
   your praxis,
   The sound of success conch will not be heard if you
   break your word.

492. The word in your mind is important for the Divine
   blessing,
   The sanctity of what you DO is of paramount
   importance,
   Everyone with a touch of need deserves your
   helping hand.

493. Arguments No, Rivalry No, the Welfare of all is the
   need,
   Let good happen instead of harm, don't try to
   degrade anyone,
   Compassion is good, grace is great and problems
   will fly off.

494. No snobbery in the attire of the learned, simpilicity
   suffices,
   Put-on pomp will dump us, contentment will show
   the light,
   Reach the desired destination treading the path
   shown by your teacher.

495. Imagine the Divine and achieve with patience,
Let Divinity flourish in your thinking,
That indeed is the transcendental Divinity.

496. Let the heaviness of words go down and away,
The value of ideas will multiply when shared,
Scatter the Divine light and depend on the strength
of cognition.

497. As the strong should always help the have-nots,
The wise man should show the greedy the right
path,
The right quality and strength of action ensure
success.

498. The cultivator and the hard worker should derive
their benefit,
Do your work well with attention and without any
shortfall.
The benefit should be decent for one's work
whether of body or of mind.

499. Social justice is the first step to the betterment of
society,
Keeping this step strong coupling economic justice
is an asset,
The step of cultural justice is the defining feature of
human existence.

500. The rich should recognize the value of the wealth
creation,
The distributors should recognize the investment of
the labour,
Those who consume should not ignore those who
supply.

501. Anger spreads dirt around and forgiveness cleans it
up,
Untruth will spoil the scene, truth will rectify the
situation,
The three pronged thispact purity is the
nourishment for all.

502. Ignorance is the source of all evil qualities,
Untruth will dry us up from all angles,
The flames of deceit will burn us down.

503. Hear, comprehend and develop self-sufficiency,
The tradition of connecting is good for all,
The tradition of segregation is harmful.

504. The terrifier will drag you to perdition,
The tempting converter will go to hell,
Meet,listen, ideate if you like, but be at ease.

505. Realize the Divinity beyond the temple,
Realize the knowledge beyond the school,
Transcend money and share with generosity.

506. Logical churning gives us the butter of higher truth,
The passion of myness will harm from all angles,
Don't get stuck with your thinking, evaluvate it
    with logic.

507. Change the wrong habits, good will be the result,
Do not worry about what you cannot obliterate,
As the tree so the fruit, as the mindset so the
    thoughts.

508. The new beggar does not know the right time,
New money and New power brook no manners,
Knowing one's limits is ideal, not knowing causes
    distractions.

509. You should not be like 'I flounder but I blame
    others',
Your estimate is yours, then why blame others,
Observe properly, evaluate correctly and decide
    firmly.

510. Discuss today's guess with yourself in your mind,
Do right today today's work, don't leave it to later,
Complete today's charity today itself, good will
    result.

511. You cannot store water that has streamed off,
Make the curd right today, otherwise the milk will
    turn sour,
Doing what is DUE at the right time is the real
    DUTY.

512. A large rock can be stopped with the help of small
       stones,
     Recognize your supporters among your juniors and
       dependents,
     Strengthen yourself with the blessings of love and
       generosity.

513. Your behaviour should reflect your good intentions,
     Observe the predicaments of others in your
       hardships,
     Well,make your expedient available to others also.

514. Recognize and think of the general situation,
     Your opinion is only your point of view,
     Gather and think of the opinions of others too.

515. Sprinkle the seeds you sow in the right place
     Refer to your aphorisms where they will be heard,
     Present pleasantly and the others may listen to you.

516. No fruit can give you strength that you have no
       access to,
     Use the strength you have access to, good will be
       the result,
     Strengthen the hands of others who are in need of
       your help.

517. Confrontation among the rich should not fascinate
       you,
     Unless asked for don't go forward and proffer advice,
     Give impartial advice and observe cool detachment.

518. Notice the oscillation and force in other's looks,
      Goodwill, diligence and commitment should be
          reflected in your looks,
      The one who listens to your words listens
          attentively and accepts.

519. Love can cross very high mountain ranges,
      Love can easily stand many sharp arrows,
      Love can turn the anger of others into good will.

520. Don't become a lousy jack of all trades,
      Don't ignore today's work worrying about tomorrow.
      You are the monarch of your responsibilities,
          remember,

521. Know that inappropriate words are never helpful,
      Know that hurting others is harmful,not
          one-upmanship,
      It is good to keep yourself on the right track all the
          time.

522. Having and not having should not decide your state
          of mind,
      Take care of your kinsmen and friends to the extent
          you can,
      Take care of your family responsibilities
          comprehensively.

523. Listen patiently to the words and advice of others,
      Accept words that are useful to all people
      Practice welfare with energy and grit,you will excel.

524. Just because you are strong don't trap others to
          subjugate,
      You yourself may sink along with the foolish trap,
      Relationship, propriety and humility are the real
          beacons.

525. Patting smile, helping hand, supporting shoulder,
      Enlightening wisdom, filling food,healing herbs,
      If you use them well, you will be dear to one and all.

526. Smart one has no ill feeling and is not in any type of
          debt,
      Smart one has the ability to help haves and have-nots,
      Smart one knows the value of satisfaction without
          faction and friction.

527. The custard obtained from others does not fit in,
      The porridge self earned is enough, note it,
      Your words and deeds are more precious than your
          apparel.

528. Never get into an argument with a fool,
      Don't seek an alliance with a wicked person,
      Choose the company of people committed to work
          and truth.

529. Friendship based on motiveless reciprocity is safe,
      Digestible self-earned food is safe and nourishing,
      Discussion of a known subject is safe and
          enlightening.

                                    Vennelakanti Prakasam

530. Choose a place which is well-equipped for your job,
      Do not take up anything which you cannot handle,
      Choose to use words meaningfuly and palatably.

531. No point in seeking the help of someone who
            cannot give it,
      No point in blaming the one who doesn't fulfil his
            promises,
      No point in taking up what cannot be rightly
            achieved, right?

532. Know that nothing can be done with just prayers,
      Prayers are only a support, your effort is the main
            thing,
      Your sedulousness precedes others' advice and
            god's blessing.

533. The silence of arrogance is silence of a corpse,
      Context-sensitive speech is irrevocably valuable,
      Lack of conscious effort is harmful from all angles.

534. Money-driven bragging may lead to a begging bag,
      Greed-driven deviance will dry up peace and
            calmness,
      Age-driven friedship and alliance are slick and
            dandy.

535. Conceit and lethargy will place us in peril,
      Courtesy postures should vary to suit the recipient,
      Seek the shade to steer off the scorch of the sun.

536. Be brave and work hard during difficult times,
While in plenty, be gentle and be helpful
No showing off, and crossing limits never.

537. Surrendering to Satan will not result in satiation,
Worship without work will not work for anyone,
Words without the weight of meaning will lose
their value.

538. With the udder of education the butter and bread
are yours,
If you have pleasant mind the cream of milk is yours,
Seek, strive, toil and what you need you will get.

539. Monetary wealth will shine in the company of
character wealth,
Cattle wealth will grow if you work very hard to
keep them fed,
Ideational wealth will grow wth guides well followed.

540. Where education flourishes, gentleness will
accompany,
Where love fills the heart, happiness will accompany,
If words are clear and sober, friends will accompany.

541. Harsh words from a friend, a real one,
Tempting sweetness from a buddy, a fake one,
The one who wishes well all the time is your life
partner.

          Vennelakanti Prakasam

542. Don't you ever do anything before right moment,
      Don't you ever pluck a fruit before it is ripe,
      Don't burden the children with responsibility
         before they are sixteen.

543. Don't undertake to do what you cannot handle,
      Don't you give a lecture on what is not your expertise,
      Why regret trusting the people you don't really
         know.

544. Keep away from people who indulge in fault-finding,
      Don't get misled by people who indulge in cursing,
      Without right experience don't indulge in
         comparison.

545. Let not mistakes creep in while doing your duty,
      Steering the spousal life is worthy duty,
      Raising children with discipline is filial duty.

546. For writing,grip on language and meaning are
         basic,
      In a battle, use of weapons and assessment of the
         foe are basic,
      For all acts attention, courage and clarity are basic

547. When required, taking a loan is not wrong,
      While paying back missing the intended date is
         wrong,
      Then value decreases and friendship bond will
         weaken.

548. Don't brag keeping the locational strength in mind,
Don't bargain for things you don't desire to buy,
Don't indulge in wasteful blabbery aimlessly.

549. Meaningless laughter will bring shame on you,
Meaningless anger will invite harshness,
Meaningless bragging will lead to ludicrous
situations.

550. A businessman, even for profit, he is doing
commodity servce,
Hospitals, even for earning, are rendering health
service,
Helpers, even for salary, are doing daily service.

551. Ekalavya's thumb, Dronacharya head,
Drishtadyumna's neck reflect the fruits of action,
No one can escape the action -and –reaction cycle;
think and ponder.

552. Your nature is paramount, not your money and
property,
Your legitimate earning route is appreciable in
many ways,
Your deviant earning route is regrettable from all
angles.

553. Every being is the protagonist of their own story,
You are of course the hero of your own story,
Treat others with respect and success will be yours.

554. Your devotion, your strength, your tact constitute
        your core self,
     You should not be led to the strength and property
        of others,
     Skill will give us composition and things will give us
        the product.

555. If money is main, the priest is in trouble,
     If fees is main, the doctor is in danger,
     If bragging is main, the guide cannot gain.

556. Seedling, water and manure are important if the
        crop finds a field,
     Teacher, book and discussion are important if the
        scholar has attention,
     Doors, walls and windows are important if the
        house has a roof.

557. Ignorant devotion does not take us across,
     Uncomprehended ideas are not knowledge,
     Distracted way will not lead us to destination.

558. To your brother and father will be equal your
        husband if you are smart,
     To your mother and sister will be equal your wife if
        you are smart,
     Word, act, gift and help if context-sensitive you are
        smart.

559. Withhold unpalatable words there will not be any
        quarrel,
      Set aside unwelcome actions there will be no
        clash,
      Smile, patience and balance are necessary for
        symbiosis.

560. If your tongue slips, it is risky for both your face
        and back,
      If you slip the wrong way the body can be in danger,
      If you slip in your looks take appropriate steps.

561. Passion and ego may lead to conflict,
      Discernment and liking may create a lead for love,
      Friendship and altruism may yield you sobriquet of
        CHEERY.

562. Don't you ever develop rivalry with others,
      Don't practise hostility with anyone,
      Love yourself and others equally taking them as
        yours.

563. Do not stay at a place for too long where there is no
        value,
      Don't be lavish in your speech where you don't have
        a standing,
      Don't you try many things where good results do
        not come forth.

 Vennelakanti Prakasam

564. Carry the strength of character, abandon the weight
of indebtedness,
Don't end up as character-free but end up as
debt-free,
Cover your recognition with appreciation and right
demeanour.

565. The value of a village is reflected in the trader's
routine glow,
To the tree, to the weed, to the man and to the clay
water is the glow,
For the writer, for the speaker and the teacher word
power is glow.

566. The educated will shine with his self-discipline and
virtous behaviour,
The merchant will shine with quality of goods and
affordable prices,
The officer will shine with his helpful decisions and
impartiality.

567. What is the use of educaton if you cannot clear
doubts,
What is the use of spectacles if the sight is not
improved,
What is the use of punishment if it cannot reform
the offender.

568. Devotion is not devotion if it increases hatred for
     others,
     Food is not food if it does not sate the appetite and
     digest,
     Father is not father if he doesn't encourage and
     show the right path.

569. Give up what you cannot chew and choose
     something else,
     Give up the language you can't handle and go back
     to mother tongue,
     Which is pleasant to the ear and meanings are easy
     to grasp.

570. Choose right path to reach the destination,
     Choose the right time to take up and succeed,
     Choose the right method to get the work done fast.

571. In mind gentleness, in behavior humility fit in,
     In mind goodness, in behaviour civility fit in,
     In mind fearlessness, in behavior equanimity fit in.

572. Relize the oneness in living beings and invariance
     in human beings,
     Realize the inseparability between the individual
     and the Supreme being,
     Realize the inseparable bond between the
     individual and the Society.

    Vennelakanti Prakasam

573. Don't accept unquestioningly what someone else
      writes,
    Think, discern, receive what appeals to you,
    Compare things and then make the correct choice.

574. Recognize the goodness in you and accept others as
      yours,
    Evaluate what you have done and tread the chosen
      path,
    Take others' cooperation but mind you, the
      responsibility is yours.

575. The main thing is not how much you have with you,
    See how many employees you can provide
      livelihood,
    See nothing is wasted and share with others correctly.

576. Your breath is the base for your existence,
    Your thinking is the fuel for your being,
    Your activity is the illustration for your living.

577. What others do does not reflect you,
    Your plan for the action of others reflects you,
    Idea, strategy, investment are yours and also of
      others.

578. Panic does not touch the one without arrogance,
    Do as much as you can of the work you got to do,
    Be blessed, realize you are not responsible for
      success or failure.

579. The real fruit of knowledge is the realization of
      oneness,
      When there is no otherness, fear has no place to
      come in,
      Transcedning the dualities without 'me' and 'they'
      feeling is salvation.

580. Ignorance has no limits but it has prejudices,
      Ignorance encourages myness and the bragging
      gets us into problems,
      Only love and affection touch them who brook no
      biases.

581. Light may reduce due to the darkness but won't
      vanish,
      Summon courage to fight on, difficulties will
      disappear,
      The ambrosia of experience will eliminate all the
      impediments.

582. The ignoramus will face difficulties if the patience
      to learn is absent,
      If the value of the self is seen in the value of the
      Supreme,
      The pot of ignorance will break and the oneness of
      beings will shine

583. Respect the seniors as if they are parents,
      Love the companions as if they are siblings,
      Treat the youngsters as if they are your children.

584. To comprehend a new subject a lot of worldiness is
        important,
     To lecture for an hour you need three hours of
        preparation,
     During difficult times do favourite things and
        achieve calmness.

585. Keep away an imbecile fellow and a fraud,
     Show the correct path to naive and young person,
     Become close to the knower who can guide you.

586. With right words and heartiness, anything is
        possible.
     If your effort is strong,fortune favours you,
     If you keep sharing what you have,it will expand.

587. With marble capture the good done by others,
     Hide in the sand the bad done by others,
     Forgive the doer,forget the hurt but archive the
        incident.

588. Forsake fear, it should not become your life style,
     Raise your contentment,, lower your brag and share
        your positivity,
     You are not the causer, doing is important, not
        tension about result.

589. Silence is welcome where you are the donor,
     Clarity is important where you are the recipient,
     What you can, don't talk of it, do it and show.

590. What you know is of value when others also share
        it,
     What you say has value when others accept it,
     What you have promised has value if it is done.

591. If not removable, cover up your mistakes,
     Correct the mistakes you have covered up once,
     If others are harmed, those mistakes will become
        sins.

592. Faultless ideas will elevate you,
     Faultless wheedling will please you,
     Faultless activity will fetch you fame.

593. When needed raising a loan is in order,
     But that much which can be paid back in time,
     While lending see it's not a big loss if unreturned.

594. Hostility should not ever be there in you,
     If others have hostility it is their problem,
     It will melt off with time and your calmness.

595. Time is precious to maintain proper relation,
     It is with time our life stream flows forward,
     At every stage be prepared for the situation that
        crops up.

596. Let the good qualities in you bloom well,
     You are the center of your universe, love and strive,
     What you want to have will seek and reach you.

Vennelakanti Prakasam

597. Don't fade fast wailing for what is lost,
     It will come back to you pretty soon,
     You have to only strive with focus and dedication.

598. With your skill achieve the much needed change,
     Circumstances will favour you and the functioning
        will be easy,
     Give appropriate value to others' fruitful hardwork.

599. Enhance your strength with tact and smile,
     Don't set aside difficult work if you like it,
     Don't get exhausted,take others' help if need be.

600. See beauty everywhere and identify the positive,
     Fill in every word with sweetness of meaning,
     Fill in every work the ambrosia of altruism.

601. It is an illusion that one can get the fruit without
        hard work,
     Grabbing money from others without being caught
        is also work,
     Putting in necessary work and reaping the needed
        fruit is the real toil.

602. Meaningless chatter is harmful both ways,
     Truthful words do good and bear fruit,
     Adequate reward for your work is comforting.

603. What is indifferent and altruistic is light mind,
     The light mind ends up as the sinless mind,
     Noncarnality and happy living are achievable.

604. Your mind directing your body condition is correct,
Guide your mind properly when it is catering to
needs of the body,
Your tasty food should strengthen your body and
thinking.

605. Proper ideation will show you the right path.
Correct path will guide you to the chosen goal,
The goal for us, not just you, is emancipation.

606. Self-dug pit no one can really complain about,
Seeking a faultless friend will make you friendless,
If you conceal your problems you cannot get others'
help.

607. Those who praise you and slander others,
Later will praise others and slander you,
Don't go by rumours and don't encourage slander.

608. Criticism before you though hurting is profitable,
Praise before you though pleasing will harm you
later,
Discussion of subject matter is better than
discussion of people.

609. Old teachers and new books are a good combination,
Reading requires understanding to become
knowledge,
Experience is a must to achive awareness, right?

                                    Vennelakanti Prakasam

610. A river, wherever it starts, is great when it irrigates
       crops,
    A person, whatever be the background, is great if
       useful to others,
    An idea,whosesoever it may be, is great if helpful to
       many people.

611. Chew well each lump there will no indigestion,
    Negotiate each step separately you will not be tired,
    Do each task carefully and there will be no lapse.

612. The wellfilled pot does not rock,
    The fully served leaf does not flutter,
    The one who knows well keeps calm.

613. Do not estimate any item's value by looking at its
       price,
    Estimate and bargain when the real value is known,
    Knowing the burden of emotion, weigh your words
       and use.

614. The one who is mighty and bold is like a lion,
    Only if it is needed he gets ready to confront,
    Fights, wins and maintains silence coolly.

615. Gentleness shines while conversing with fellow
       passengers,
    Truthfulness shines while dealing with fellow
       traders,
    Friendship shines glowingly in the case of spousal
       mates.

616. The milk in a friend's pot will curdle if salt of fear
        sets in,
     The functioning of an office will get disturbed if the
        bells of power ring in,
     The bond of friendship will get disturbed if
        suspisicion is set in

617. If you look for faultless friends the result will be
        zero,
     If negativity is totally unwelcome marriages also
        will not take place,
     If rethinking is avoided knowledge cannot be
        acquired and gained.

618. If others are troubled we too will be losers,
     Fear and hatred with negativity will do us bad,
     Love and meditation with sobriety will do us good.

619. Ignoring others and keeping yourself off, no one
        will remember you,
     Wishing bad for others is bad and you will get only
        bad results,
     Wishing good to others is noble and you will reap
        right dividends.

620. Solidify the nest of love with all twigs in place,
     Protect your house of fame and let no hole isolate
        you,
     You are the hero, villain and the protective shield of
        your story.

                                    Vennelakanti Prakasam

621. The rays of the sun can pierce the darkness,
Shiny words can break even iron chains,
Words can break down enmity if they are truthful
   and gentle.

622. By working together responsibility gets centralized,
The food item will have single name even if the
   ingredients are many,
Even the slavish link will shine if love is there.

623. The love flower blooms in spring but never withers
   away,
Envy and suspicion will never jell with love,
The reward for love is the anointment of Agape.

624. The value of shade canot be realized without the
   impact of the sun,
The value of food can be realized by knowing the
   pangs of hunger,
The value of friendship can't be realized without
   the affliction of loneliness.

625. Do not stop the power of action as long as you breathe,
Charities should not be stopped as long as the
   means are available,
Do not stop the desire to learn as long as your
   cognition is active.

626. The stairs of the past should not be forgotten,
The route for the terrace of present are those steps,
The same are the props for tomorrow's growth.

627. When interests meet we become close,
      Needs also bring us close to one another,
      Use the opportunities for peer friendship.

628. Dream new dreams for the new year,
      Give functional footwear for those dreams,
      Good ideas should accompany functionality.

629. Think coolly to foster and boost strong positivity,
      That strength will reach you through the rays of
          intellection,
      You are blessed if you can share with others your
          positivity.

630. Silence is a way to observe and ruminate about good,
      Peace is the state to think and decide about good
          deeds,
      Modesty is the best route to increase the sharing of
          good results.

631. Tact to power, intelligence to success are good
          company,
      Experience, perseverance and discernment should
          join hands,
      If you want to help others, you have to use altruist
          wisdom.

632. Good can be seen if evil can be endured,
      Show your intellect in deeds, not just in words,
      Impress the good by cleverly disrobing the evil.

                                    Vennelakanti Prakasam

633. The bird may come back and be yours,
Remember that the word blurted out will not come
        back,
Think and let only harmless words come out of you.

634. It is natural for any being to feel pain when it is hurt,
The smartness is in not letting the hurt be repeated,
It is good if you do not let yourself hurt others.

635. Let not the tongue represent what is not seen,
Let not the mind ponder what is not heard,
Don't fib about what you have not touched and nor
        tasted.

636. If you lose by telling the truth no harm,
If you gain by telling the lie is very bad,
If you gain back by telling the truth wonderful.

637. Don't celebrate the fall of your enemy.
Keep away, need not lend your support,
If there is a way to reduce resentment, do reduce.

638. Let the deserving person get what is due,
But do not give someone who does not deserve it,
All help and charity should for the deserving, Right?

639. Do not hanker after what you don't deserve,
As fruit worthy of work, seek deed deserving fame,
Seeds of fame are in sharing and in praising

640. Learning is truly an eternal and ongoing activity,
The ocean of knowledge does not share any shore,
Ignorance has no limits but will bear plenty of
prejudices.

641. Don't harm someone by wrong blaming, the fall
will be closeby,
Increase the value of the good that exists, better
will follow,
Weigh it, good always has great value anywhere,
anytime.

642. The most sacred lake is your mind,
The most sacred armour is your body,
The most sacred power is love for fellow beings.

643. Dictatorship can be a bed for many a heinous
crime,
Righterous is the polity that seeks overall welfare,
Dividing work and sharing the fruit is the Divine
path.

644. The true temple is the womb which is the basis of
creation,
You are a god who came out of that womb,
Don't let self-centeredness subdue that primordial
Divinity.

645. Blessed are they who own up their mistakes,
Righteous are they who correct their mistakes and
atone,
Divine beings are they who know right from wrong
and guide people well.

646. Self-slander is forbidden, self-praise is unacceptable,
Backing the good, bending the bad and moving
forward is justifiable,
Righteous it is to be aware of all the routes and
giving guidance.

647. Awareness of rectitude is the first step for an
enlightened one,
Protecting the self and others and ciceroning is the
second step,
The third step is to use the opportunity to fullfill
others' needs.

648. Analysis of collected data leads to intellection
creating knowledge,
Knowing the limits of knowledge, the wise create
flashes of awareness,
They who use their intellect to do good to others
are righteous folks.

649. Content collection, knowledge development and
intellectual churning,
Use all these for the development of self and others
If there is no 'other' in the society the 'self' cannot
be built.

650. The expert is one step higher than the knower,
      The intellectual is one step higher than the expert,
      The wise man is one step higher than the intellectual.

651. The geniuses transcend their sociopolitical
         identities,
      They always try to show the way to know the
         unknown,
      The true genius does not succumb to the riches of
         office.

652. The genius of growth seeks silence and serenity,
      Ego does not reach the real genius who knows the
         limits,
      The words of a genius are the paths of knowledge
         for us.

653. Experience, discernment and silence are the
         qualities of a genius,
      Rapport with logic will engender diverse
         significations,
      Even with diverse significations the genius knows
         his shore.

654. Comment is unnecessary for the work you do,
      There must be reasons for the undoables you are
         doing,
      Work which need not be hidden is good work,
         right?

                                    Vennelakanti Prakasam

655. Don't be a cause for the anger of every smiling
      gentleman,
      Don't be the prop for someone who seeks to weild
      power,
      Don't be a witness for the one who treads the path
      of crime.

656. Answer any question only after the anger subsides,
      Don't leave the good path, you can teach others
      ethics,
      Finish the work you have in hand with what you
      have.

657. You are Jnanayogi when people seek your guidance
      in many fields,
      You are Karmayogi if you are able to do each task
      attentively,
      You are Bhakthiyogi if setting aside other things
      you just meditate.

658. You can't get a pole out of seed, wasteful activity,
      If the value of the substance is not known you
      cannot make a snack of it,
      If you don't know the value of a thing you cannot
      bargain correctly.

659. Unnecessary anger, prattle and unprogressive
      change,
      Know that they will not work for anyone anyway,
      Know the value of the person and avoid goalless
      drudging.

660. The ignorant groups do not choose the path of
     patience,
     Those who can't visualise new things don't want
     change,
     Those who do not know how to cook can't become
     culinarians.

661. The worm that grows on dung is harmful in all
     respects,
     The arrogance that grows in the ignorant is doubly
     detrimental,
     No correct path can be chosen with superficial
     knowledge.

662. Our problems lose weight when we view others'
     problems,
     Know the value, price and available cash before buying,
     Do not argue with strong opponents about the
     unknown.

663. Good intentions must precede bold adventure,
     Find out if water is coming to the farm before buying it,
     Know your stamina and weight before competing.

664. The ignoramus should always step back,
     The tactful knower should step forward,
     Only then the intended task can be achieved.

665. The benefactor is the real rich man of virtue,
     The one who is greedy is actually the poor guy,
     The nonsmart who cannot speak clenches the fist.

                                    Vennelakanti Prakasam

666. Distancing does not increase feeling of mutuality,
     Argument cannot be reflective of sanity,
     Quarrelling is not the base for strength and tact.

667. The potter is short of pots for use, it is said,
     The carpenter's door is badly set up, it is said,
     We should not ignore our own needs while serving
         others.

668. The envious will perish and the greedy will become
         needy,
     Enough benefit to the two categories if they want
         the best for all,
     The mind of the teacher sharpens while teaching
         the students.

669. Wealth steps in with dignity while entering,
     Wealth runs out in a hurry while leaving,
     Vigilance is the backbone for the future.

670. Regretting after hasty and nonfruiting work is not
         welcome,
     Reaping the right fruit after slow and steady work is
         welcome,
     Whatever we do and whatever we say should fit in
         well, right?

671. Fellow workers should meet as if siblings,
     Different aspects of work should be skilfully
         dovetailed,
     There should not be any lapse in behoving and
         rewarding.

672. There is danger of the rope of falsehood breaking off,
The hawser of truth can survive for many seasons,
Remember that the work being done should stay
    for long.

673. If the secret is spelled out multiple disruptions may
    result,
Decreased water content can cause the crop to dry
    off.
Water for crop, privacy for the family are of
    paramount value.

674. Humour adds grace to our life journey,
without verve in your nerve work will not reach its
    peak,
Strength and attention are necessary, cheerfulness
    will co-glow.

675. Education is important but experience is very
    essential,
Sourness and spiciness are necessary but salty
    touch is essential,
Your body needs food and your frame needs
    correct dress.

676. A betraying friend is more dangerous than a
    declared foe,
A digestable lump of food is better than unknown
    special dish,
Ignoring the external finish choose the ones that
    will help you.

677. The nature fixes the rain bond between the earth
          and sky,
      Without rain the earth will not give us crops,
      Nature will give us fruits only with human effort.

678. Nature's energy is stored in the box of silence,
      Words give us only emotional reflections,
      Achieve clarity of mind before using words.

679. Wealth is not the core asset to the wealthy,
      Righ company is important for Divine prosperity,
      Strengthen the mind with silence and it will shine.

680. Let the light in you outglow the social glow,
      Only then can the Divinity in you will emerge,
      The words of others are your paths, your words are
          their paths.

681. Without surrendering to power think differently,
      It's not defiance, it's just blooming of new ideas,
      If six upon ten, becoming new ideator is in order.

682. At the age of seven we start noticing the
          surroundings,
      At the age of sixteen one is skilled for new ideated
          action,
      Each person is a scholar if he promotes his passion
          well.

683. Physicality is for existence, psychicness is for
       humanity,
    Humanness is for cosmic consciousness and
       awareness,
    Without transcending boundaries Divinity cannot
       be attained.

684. The yearning, not rest, helps in Divine attainment,
    Transcending materialism is the goal of one's
       existence,
    The soul does not seek rest, the purpose of soul is
       to attain the Divine.

685. Work for body is very much like animal labour,
    The work for society qualifies to be human work,
    Awareness of the universal consciousness is the
       ultimate.

686. Recognize the power within you and add strength,
    Achieve then the recognition by others,
    If your energy and strength are for others it is
       Divinity.

687. While coming hands were empty, not the state of
       mind,
    Observe, comprehend, learn and share,
    What you know share well, empty yourself.

688. Don't get struck in a corner, move out towards
          awareness,
     Sow new seed, your experience is your fertiliser and
          water,
     Grow up in every matter as knower supreme.

689. Resistence strengthens and emboldens the
          wounded mind,
     Resistence needs support from discretion and
          comraderie,
     Resistence should be meaningful and gentleness
          should accompany.

690. When you give up your needs and rights you will
          mature,
     The leader has less freedom and more responsibility,
     Specific purpose, purity of goal and pure speech are
          a must.

691. Your sweat should provide water for others,
     Your muscle should provide protection to others,
     Your word should be prop for others and should
          guide them.

692. Do not let an alien culture replace your own culture,
     Do not let someone else's language displace your
          own language,
     Tread new path with your own cognizance and
          enhance the result.

693. Know the charm of society and individuals,
     Only equality can conserve the societal value,
     Patience and self-reliance embody values in human
          beings.

694. Environmental cleanliness sharpens the mind,
     Mental cleanliness increases spiritual creativity,
     Creativity in all fields strengthens human progress.

695. Share your love with the downtrodden, they need it,
     Provide skills to the unskilled, they can become self
          employed,
     Explain to the ignoramus the value of the thispact
          purity.

696. Far away cows have indeed long horns,
     The new recipes are always attractive,
     But home is the best and home food is the best.

697. Silence is better than saying the wrong thing,
     Nonbuying is better than buying unnecessary
          things,
     Adequate walk is better than wrongly done yoga.

698. Do not neglect poor friends and minor injuries,
     Do not neglect small debts and promises made,
     Do not neglect the anger of the menials and your
          own lapses.

                                      Vennelakanti Prakasam

699. Friendship increases happiness and dilutes sorrow,
    Stay away from the arrogance engendered by
        money,
    Turn the authority of office into concerned
        responsibility.

700. A friend's slap pains the face but will be a help to
        you,
    The false compliment of a foe is feast for your ears
        but bad for you,
    Find different sweet and tactful ways to turn a foe
        into a friend.

701. Details of your wealth others need not know,
    The turns and twists of your thinking others need
        not know,
    Your plan of action others need not know except to
        help you.

702. Brevity is said to be the soul of wit,
    Adequate food provides needed nutrition
    Adequate exertion strengthens the body and
        nourishes the mind.

703. The work done systematically will fructify in time,
    Deviant means cause loss of time and damage
        quality,
    Better to take rest and study what can be
        comprehended.

704. Whatever you can do is better than what others can
         do for you,
      The money you have has more value than the
         money to arrive,
      The poor friend with you is of greater value than
         distant rich friend.

705. Don't worry about spilled milk,
      Don't worry about the unattained position,
      Do what you can and be pleased with the
         buttermilk you have.

706. Wish to be an independent being in a small hut,
      Wish not to be a small worker in a big building,
      Your ideas are of more value than someone else's
         treasure.

707. The modus operandi is more important than the
         victory celebration,
      You are the boss of your responsibilities and others
         are just helpers,
      You are the hero of your life journey,others are side
         artists.

708. No stopping of shot bullet or released word,
      Beware your game is over if you have wronged,
      Speak less and weigh your words,be careful.

709. One who is attentive is good for your work
     More than five people who are not attentive,
     Choose the one who is fond of work and the work
        will be done.

710. If you unduly rest in summer,
     Food may be denied in spring,
     Better work when you can work.

711. Knowing adults are guides to the youngsters,
     Haves are the pioneering guides to the have-nots,
     The excelling ones should be real models.

712. Blessed are they who correct their wrongs,
     Blessed are they who show their skill and help,
     Blessed are they who reduce their anger with a smile.

713. Faith and hope are okay but not greed,
     Caution and alertness are okay but not fear and
        anxiety,
     Love and respect are okay but not infatuation.

714. Realize the purpose of what is read,
     Reconcile the contents in what is written,
     Relevance and commitment should be reflected in
        what is said.

715. There can be no fragrance in self praise,
     Not everything is true in invectives,
     One should disceern the weaving of bad and good
        to decide.

716. Realize the value of time, don't waste it,
     Know the value of food, take adequately,
     Do whatever is due at the right moment.

717. Screaming for peace is of no avail,
     Tolerate with peace and live in peace,
     Strangers can embrace peace if they see it in you.

718. Show love and respect for fellow beings,
     Then they can return love and respect,
     What you can't give away, others can't give you.

719. The foundation for our homes is a blend of
         ancestral sweat and blood,
     The property we inherit is a blend of labour and
         savings of the ancestors,
     To give to our heirs we have to work hard and save
         silently.

720. Participating in the discussion of ideas is sattvic,
     Participating in the discussion of events is rajasic,
     Participating in the discussion of individuals is
         tamasic.

721. Your glory is the crown that society gives you,
     Defend the reputation with selfless activity,
     Defend the crown and avoid being whipped.

722. The quality of your thoughts will determine your
        well-being,
      Truthfulness of your words will determine the level
        of your success,
      The selfless service in your actions will determine
        the level of reputation.

723. Be useful to others with what you have.
      Be content with the recognition you get and do
        more service,
      Know that the real work is what you do for others,

724. The rain beginning with a single drizzle is the
        nature of clouds,
      Evaporation of sea water into clouds is the nature of
        the Sun,
      Starting for the place you have chosen and reaching
        it is your nature.`

725. Change is natural, don't get fooled by opposing
        change,
      Join hands with change skilfully and achieve success,
      Decision to do or not to do is driven by
        circumstances.

726. There is no gain in wailing over the past,
      There is nothing we can do by worrying about the
        future,
      Do your duty today and be satisfied with what you
        have.

727. Why should you breed the weed with anxiety,
     Grow the crop with confidence and perseverance,
     Turn problems into opportunities, success will
          result.

728. Customize yourself with your thoughts,
     Nurture what you think is fit for you,
     Create for yourself what you can imagine.

729. Hear in silence the cosmic flow, the cosmic music,
     Immerse yourself in meditation with detachment,
     Knowledge of the Divine is the only goal that you
          will enjoy.

730. Yesterday will lead to today along with results of
          action,
     Set right your today and achieve detachment,
     The result of tomorrow's action will be blissful.

731. Solve the problem, abandon if difficult,
     Nothing can be achieved with sadness and disgust,
     With firmness choose a new path and move ahead.

732. If compassion is your nature your social status has
          no problem,
     If attention and aptitude are your tools failure has
          no place,
     If you are close to your goal, success has no
          alternative.

733. Sometimes not getting what you want is matter of
        luck,
     Sharpen some other task and achieve it, good will
        result,
     Do not let life get you down with unnecessary
        worries.

734. Compassion is the source of happiness for you and
        others,
     Knowledge is the source of immortality for you and
        others,
     Share your knowledge with others, they will always
        remember you.

735. Weave a brave armour with experience and smart
        planning,
     Hope is a big pillar to gain fulfillment on all fronts,
     The shield and pillar will help you to reach your
        goal.

736. There is no need to choose the path for happiness,
     You should know happiness is the real path of life,
     Love, forgiveness and piety are the tone, tune and
        the timbre of the path.

737. Don't you ever worry about the mire of grief,
     Without the mire of experience, your heart will not
        blossom,
     The blossoming lotus gives you energy in the
        sunlight.

738. The rythm in your gait will bring peace to others,
      Be close to the earth and march forward,
      No fear and no force, fairness is enough to reach
         the goal.

739. Watch carefully, push aside the anxiety of result,
      What awareness shows is the path of action,
      The path of action is the basis for you and the
         scepters.

740. Your faith will save you all the time, it won't let you
         down,
      The attention and desire you have will provide the
         needed format,
      What you get is your self-earned pearl of success.

741. No one should ask for an unchanging inanimate life,
      A selfless altruistic life is beneficial to all,
      Is it possible to have solo life without others?

742. Roads are for your journey, go ahead,
      No matter how far, don't you leave the road,
      Small steps can cross the hills and help you reach
         the goal.

743. Choose the job you like, the work will not strain
         you,
      Consume your favourite food and stay healthy,
      Cognize all as yours, your choices will not be
         disturbed.

744. Ruminate useful ideas, world will be in order,
     Choose a good place and your mind will blossom,
     See beauty in what you see and all will be glorious.

745. Do whatever you want to as per your goal,
     Sow the seeds fast if you want your crop,
     If there is time for the crop meanwhile go in for
          planting for forest.

746. Know that education is a vast arsenal,
     Include gentleness with enlightening education,
     Include altruism along with successful education.

747. Your faith will lead you to different ideas,
     Your ideas will lead you to words and deeds,
     With actions values are formed and with values you
          stand.

748. There is no life without activity, so lead to activity,
     Think about fruits of action, set out to act,
     Don't worry about the result and don't let fear
          succeed..

749. Power strikes wrong path, misled by fear,
     Unnecessary fault-finding is also due to fear,
     Drive away fear, know your duty and spread strength.

750. Values cannot be bought as they grow in us,
     Education and culture are the bases for that growth,
     Go forward on your own, use the stairs to reach the
          terrace.

751. Money is the source of business world,
Relation is the source for social life,
Desire and dedication are the sources for
knowledge

752. A company is not walls and vehicles, it is humans,
Inhumane business style is destructive,
Giving and receiving are integral to business.

753. To get the roses feeling the thorns is okay,
To see the rainbow you have to smile in the rain
drops,
If you want co-existential link adjustment is a must.

754. Strive hard to achieve quick and complete success,
Don't stop the work in middle fearing defeat or
failure,
Treat whatever has been done as harbinger of
success.

755. Goal is your aim and it will show you the way,
Competitors can do nothing but alerting you,
Overcoming fear, strengthening your resolve,
reach the goal.

756. Overcome superstitions and avoid rigmarole of
rituals,
Respect the trustworthy and move forward,
Logic is important and feasibility will do the job.

 Vennelakanti Prakasam

757. Full life is actually the way we live,
      The question is how purposeful it has been,
      The festival is for all not just for the self.

758. Let all people feel that the earth is heavenly,
      Let the words cognized come out for public use,
      There is no point in hiding either words or goods.

759. Transform negativity into positivity in the lake of love,
      Emptiness turns into omnipotence in the furnace of
          Truth and Agape,
      Accomplish something great for and along with
          others.

760. Let the assumptions spring up, don't thwart them,
      Let those springs stream forward, nothing to fear,
      Once ideas pool in serve them to your sharers.

761. Once the basic needs are identified and met,
      The first task is to implement what is intended,
      Your second task is to share the honey of love.

762. Use the Sun as you support and feed on the Air like
          a snake,
      Churn the chances well and receive the Butter of
          experience,
      In real life you are both the warrior and charioteer.

763. Shower affection and experience intimacy,
      Spread affection and effect elite leadership,
      Burn lethargy with your words and glow as a teacher.

764. Do not waste your inhales and exhales,
	While doing your work there should be a reason to
		rest,
	Your decision is the final decision, see it is
		acceptable.

765. Say with hope that despair does not fit nor greed,
	Tell the time that wasting is not festivity,
	Festivity means sharing the butter with others.

766. The limits to your deeds are your feelings and
		desires,
	Fix limits to your desire, share what you save,
	What you share grows, contentment grows and no
		depletion.

767. Don't impose an ending, continue your activity,
	Wait, think, experience and go ahead without
		stopping,
	You are a contributor to the community, don't be a
		burden.

768. Only with us exists our society, self-confidence is
		very important,
	Expand opportunities and make good use of them
		for societal good,
	Increase your talent, share its wings and become
		useful to others.

	

769. Your past has moulded you, your talent will mould
        the future,
      Use all your strength to build a vibrant societal
        edifice,
      Behave in a way that the future generations
        remember you.

770. Society needs your courage and your faith,
      Other people need your work and you need their
        work,
      No place for sadness, no shadow of indifference,
        move forward.

771. Evaluate the the success of others and appreciate it,
      Evaluate your own work and explain the possibility,
      Insert 'we' in 'I' and turn 'let us' into 'let's',the result
        is justice.

772. Prepare change skilfully as a stepping stone to
        success,
      Making work beneficial to many is a real success,
      Deriving strength from digested food and serving
        others is success.

773. Washing plates and bowls and making them shine
        is success,
      Washing clothes and making them look good is
        success,
      Washing the floor and achieving full cleanliness is
        success.

774. Encourage children to achieve maturity in their
     work,
     Encourage the prisoners to change and achieve
     affability,
     Every commodity has value, likewise every human
     has value.

775. Dare to reach the summit, don't hesitate,
     Understand that every step is just below the peak,
     Your strength and determination are your real
     possessions.

776. Accept what strikes you and intellect what you
     ideate,
     Sift them well and develop a theoretical frame,
     The work that a genius does is no different, you are
     a genius.

777. Put away the prejudices, your own and of others,
     Let others join you with their benign opinions,
     Don't fib, don't be nervy, step forward to reach an
     accord.

778. Keep your mind and heart open to receive and
     share,
     Shower love, share appreciation and desire peace
     and love,
     In your furnace of love turn others penury into
     affluence.

 Vennelakanti Prakasam

779. Every moment is Divine, every person is a priest,
    The one who knows his goal and has clarity about it
        is the boss,
    Lay the foundation for your work and proceed
        forward.

780. Every opportunity is a Divine blessing,
    Receive, respond and achieve what is right,
    Good should accrue to you and your partners.

781. Follow the path of grandparents and greatgrand
        parents,
    Strengthen the path, and if there is dirt clean it up,
    Endure hardship, don't deride and effect change
        skilfully.

782. Do not go to extremes and miss opportunities,
    Invite innovation as long as it leads to development,
    Recognize and appreciate the support of adults and
        friends.

783. How is it life, if you do not do what you can and
        what you should?
    Every creature must carry on its activity without
        forgetting its value,
    Otherwise it amounts to ignoring the ultimate aim
        of life.

784.	Preserve your culture and do not mock other
	cultures,
	God loves everyone and protects everyone,no
	discrimination,
	God does not go by social, economic, political
	identities.

785.	There is no other hero beyond you in your story,
	Know if you are milkman even the diamond man
	will come to you,
	If you want shoes, you will go to shoe shop not to
	the garment shop.

786.	What you give is yours, and your words are yours,
	Believe what you do for others is your work,
	What others say and do for you is their work.

787.	The sense of separation is okay if it is for their
	well-being,
	The sense of being together is okay for well-being
	of all,
	Your hardwork is for you and for all those who
	belong to you.

788.	Strew the seeds of love and sprinkle the water of
	forgiveness,
	Choose the guiding method to show the mirror of
	piety,
	Be the focal point of functionality for the
	community around you.

789   If you want to fly up become unfettered and leave
        behind what you have,
      If you want to establish new theory,the response of
        others would just matter,
      There is no need to worry about old tastes while
        making a new dish.

790. Do not be anxious about tomorrow while donating,
      While doing your job don't worry about what
        others think,
      Weigh words, compare actions and share fruits.

791. Accumulating wealth is not a big deal,
      It is great to profit in the way of righteousness,
      It is important to spend money on good things.

792. The boneless tongue is sharp and as well as strong,
      The damage done by misuse is abominably terrible,
      The value of your words is more than that of
        diamonds.

793. There is no water reservoir in the river stream,
      The niche in the stream of thought does not stay
        the same,
      The stream of thought can be theorized by pooling
        it.

794. Moderate food is good for the body and enough for
          the brain,
      Abstinence, ideational churning and light body is
          good for the mind,
      Delicious and adequate food will ensure ideation
          and intellection.

795. The graceful turns of rivers can be seen from the
          embankment,
      If you get into water you will only feel the chill and
          push,
      That experience also adds to the your knowledge of
          life's mysteries.

796. The waves of the sea sway only from the shore,
      The beauty of the mountain range is only from a
          distance,
      But you cannot get the experience unless you are
          with them.

797. Our actions are the messages of our survival for
          they are indicators,
      What others know about us is in the form of our
          deeds,
      The food that goes in comes out, your words will
          capsule your actions.

798. Golden victory is no different from self restraint,
      He is standard for himself and also model for others,
      Charitable contemplation, compassion and
          altruism are Divine.

799. Easily pleased person is multirich and is
          unlackingly compassionate,
     The hard worker can achieve anything with his own
          contentment,
     In our positive responses negativity can easily be
          decimated.

800. Strengthen your nature with the help of culture and
          elders' nurture,
     You should not let in unnecessary curves into your
          temperament.
     Every principle can be customised to suit the
          situation.

801. Weakness it is saying 'I don't make mistakes',
     Correct your mistakes and forgive others' mistakes
          and go ahead,
     Learn about your mistakes, admit them, try to
          change the result.

802. Well,fighting and crushing the enemy is heroism,
     Indeed heroism it is subduing and controlling
          desires not necessary,
     Knowing one's mistakes,correcting and atoning for
          them is true heroism.

803. Our thirst is not quenched with the sight of a mirage,
     Wisdom does not form with distant smoothness
          and no exercise,
     Our hunger will not be satisfied with the
          neighbour's cooking flavour.

804. Filled pots do not shake, the fully served leaf plates
        will not fly,
     The knower does not fall into the snare of boasting,
     The real giver donates with his actions not with just
        words.

805. Your homeland, your culture, your mother tongue
        are your sources,
     Your thoughts, your activity, your words are your
        being,
     Charity, service to parents and teachers are your
        Divine route.

806. Vanity, prejudice, ingratitude are your enemies,
     Humility, harmony, and gratitude are your scepters,
     Work, distribution of hard work, satisfaction are
        your Divine blessings.

807. Discernment, interest, fearlessness are the steps to
        your success,
     Carelessness, laziness, fear are the reasons for your
        backwardness,
     Choose the path that will determine the curve of
        your success.

808. Get engaged in your developmental work,
     Don't waste your time with slander and criticism,
     Feed and encourage others, your enthusiasm will
        increase.

                                     Vennelakanti Prakasam

809. Light the lamp and break the darkness,
      Realize that a new theory is born of a single thought,
      Discern, analyze, and explain with the necessary
          quest.

810. Your fault-finders are unworthy of your anger,
      Their coolness increases the sensible warmth in you,
      Change the flaws and think like a wise ascetic.

811. What joins us may be separated,but not what is in
          us,
      What is called real estate also changes,but not our
          nature,
      Well thought out action increases enlightened
          devotion.

812. Create for yourself favourable conditions,
      Customize and measure whatever you have,
      Fear out, tact in, with fairness recognise others'
          excellence.

813. Do not quarrel, compromise, think steadily,
      Others will agree if your thoughts reflect your
          sharing wisdom,
      The love of your cognition is the good achieveable
          for all.

814. True indeed that the use of sails is to suit the wind,
      Charities should reflect the calibre of the sharer,
      Virtue is in doing by choice rather than by
          compulsion.

815. A bit of functionality is better than too many words,
      Awareness does not dawn without crossing the
            threshold,
      Look at your peers, weigh their needs and help them.

816. Ignore needling words and speak smoothly,
      Ignore the greed of others amd share as much as
            you can,
      Bottle will increase the prattle, pause and be in peace.

817. Feel your work is worthwhile and go ahead with it,
      Take your words to be a model for others and be
            careful,
      There is no penance above truth, no shield above
            love.

818. The basis of peace of mind is friendship with others,
      Compassion shown to the suffering will satisfy you,
      Show the correct path and be good to the
            misguided.

819. Start doing the work and let it fructify in its time,
      Live as if you never know when you would leave,
      Learn life lessons as if you have a long innings.

820. It is fair that we like words according to their
            significative power,
      It should not be accepted on the basis of caste,
            creed or polity,
      Today, tomorrow, and forever take them as
            community companions.

                                    Vennelakanti Prakasam

821. See you are more qualified today than you were
          yesterday,
       You should never compete with others, it wont work,
       Heredity and Cosmocity are the foundations of
          your talent and toil.

822. Humility, modesty, and silence are the hallmarks of
          strength,
       The wise do not like to argue but prefer only to
          discuss,
       The trident of love, forgiveness, and piety will show
          you the Divine path.

823. Women's advancement is the investment for the
          society,
       Men's hardwork is a kind of divestment to society,
       The spousal love is the energy and fuel to the
          community.

824. The desire for revenge is a characteristic of the weak,
       Forgiving and moving is a characteristic of the
          strong,
       Small acts of help will become a bay of compassion.

825. Anger weakens all the good qualities in us,
       Forgiveness enhances the good qualities in us,
       Love is what leads us to the Divine curve.

826. Rust is the enemy of iron, it destroys,
       Fear is the enemy of the one who has it, it desiccates,
       Satisfied man has no enemy, happiness is the fruit.

827. The miser's wealth is like sea water,
      The wealth of the cultured is like well water,
      Wealth which is of no use to others is like a lifeless
         being.

828. Certainly not negativity only positivity is divinity,
      Saying no is not divinity,sharing what we have is,
      Boasting is not divinity, achieving equity is.

829. The Divine way is being able to turn penury into
         plenty,
      The Divine way is to share affluence harmoniously,
      The Divine way is to strive and thrive with others.

830. The ungrateful mind does not increase
         compatibility,
      The unforgiving mind does not foster harmony,
      The unappreciating mind cannot experience bliss.

831. Cool pleasant evening, warm good morning,
      Sweet discussion forum, known path of solution,
      To experience all these fill your mind with fondness.

832   Connected to the need and subject to possibility is
         right desire,
      What is needed and is subject to one's ability is
         right donation.
      What is not beyond one's capacity and is correctly
         scheduled is right work.

833. Ride to achieve good and operate for glory,
      Avoid excess and give as much as you can,
      If well viewed, there are no rivals and all are
          comrades.

834. Do not ignore the strength and efficiency in you,
      Do not ignore the helpful contributions of your
          friends,
      Do not ignore the core value of the work you are
          taking up.

835. You are weighed with your intended working
          methods,
      What you will get is whatever you can enjoy,
      Receive with contentment and enjoy, don't give up.

836. More important than the forms are Grace and
          Awareness,
      The rhetoric without Awarenes is a burden, not a
          blessing,
      For the concept of primordial there will be only
          Unity, no diversity.

837. Stability reduces the heaviness of work, ensures
          prestige,
      What gives us courage to start the work is faith,
      Work will progress well and the cicerone is
          diligence.

838 Scripture reading should be done with
        understanding,
     Discourse presentation should reflect discretionary
        awareness,
     Yoga practice bears real fruit with sensual restraint.

839. The atheist does not believe in what he cannot
        comprehend,
      He knows how to weigh human values and accept
        them,
      Unexpectedly he can walk the aisle of the Divine.

840. Discuss with others, collect the contents and
        strengthen your awareness,
      Achieve knowledge by comparing the subject frame
        with other things,
      Wisdom is the comparative understanding of
        diverse things.

841. Discard the harm done by others but remember it,
      Try to correct the damage you have done and never
        do it again,
      Others remember the harm more than the good
        you do.

842. Note it that whatever is seen is not desirable,
      Seek only what is useful for the given need,
      Don't worry if it is not feasable, ignore it.

     Vennelakanti Prakasam

843. Consistency of thinking is necessary, not inertia,
      Senses should be subdued, but no inactivity,
      Shun greed and avarice, but keep up right goals.

844. Heaven is the state of mind which you can attain,
      Hell is a flawed condition made up of your
          grumblings,
      The state will be stable, try to rectify your flawed
          condition.

845. The smooth hills do not give us light,
      The buffalos in our books do not get us milk,
      We cannot find dung cakes if we are away from dung.

846. If the Panchabhutas are in you then the universe is
          with you,
      Getting to know yourself is the first step to Self
          Realization,
      Admeasuring yourself is the next step to Self
          Transcendence.

847. You are a special star to yourself, shine in time,
      Lead others in that light, move forward,
      Every star rotates in its own orbit, identify your
          orbit.

848. Your destination is yours and the path you follow is
          yours,
      The speed you want is yours and move forward
          coolly,
      Do not change on others' advice, if you don't like.

849. Burn out your sorrows, cast out your doubts,
Don't give any room to doubts and coronate clarity,
Execute what is intended, achieve the desired goal.

850. Knowledge of useless things is not welcome,
       ignorance is okay,
Gather and solidify knowledge about what you like,
Do not forget the value of your place in this
       universe.

851. Sparrow does not fall without heavens knowing it,
Without the heavens you can't ideate, you can't tap,
Hold on to what is tapped, intellect it and cherish it.

852. Unemployment is a cursed life, go to work,
It should be good for you, good for the others,
Only then will your life have a certain value.

853. Poverty is not yours, but laziness is yours,
Poverty can be eradicated with money,
Laziness can be overcome with your effort.

854. Recognize your merit and shun inferiority complex,
With tact enhance the power of your action,
Use your money, money should not use you.

855. Do not mock the youngsters, praise them,
Evil eye is of no value, your confidence has all the
       value,
The courage and the stability of youth will be of
       great help.

856. If in problems seek help and offer help,
Give company to those who were with you in happy
days,
Deliberate with others the theories known and
fortify your ideation.

857. Yoga in work is skill, yoga in thought is logic,
Yoga in confidence is lack of fear, yoga in happiness
is lack of greed,
Yoga in glee and glow is good relationship with others.

858. The good small can do what the big cannot do,
A major storm can lead to a major catastrophe,
A pleasant smile with a graceful look can undo a
major damage.

859. The blacksmith's hammer gives form to iron,
The same hammer can shatter the fine glass,
It is safe to adjust to circumstances and needs.

860. Turn a difficult task into a favourite task,
Obstacles can be overcome and new milestones can
be set,
You can achieve anything if you think hard and
work well.

861. Incorporate in yourself the change you want to see
in others,
New opportunities arise, new opportunities obtain,
Nine-tenth is your effort, only one tenth is
supervention.

862. My thought is the source of my existence,
My perseverance and my awareness are the wheels,
The captain is myself, the Awareness in me.

863. The source of money is for transactions and business,
The source of curiosity is for the blooming of
	human intellect,
The source of all success is righteous courage, verily so.

864. Practice is the pillar of all learning,
Perseverance is the binding wall for all deeds,
Optimism is the hope of happiness at all times.

865. Do the good which others are blamed for not doing,
Instead of weighing others add strength to them
	and see,
Be calm and shine like the sun in the society.

866. Achieving an object useful to all is great,
Establishing a wealth creating profession is great,
Replacing ignorance with solid knowledge is great.

867. Perfection as a goal is of paramount importance,
Achievable it is unlikely in everyday life,
Keep it before you and set out on your activity trip.

868. You are no less than anyone, wrong to think you are,
Your work has its own worth, as a doer your worth
	is greater,
A little compassion and a little gentleness to convey
	your superiority.

		Vennelakanti Prakasam

869. None of your talents can be diminished, stand firm,
     Achieve the impossible and prove your operational
        talent,
     The youngsters need courage and stability about
        their talents.

870. Assume you are a happy being, no one can
        diminish your happiness,
     Happiness is your sense of talent, instinct and
        fruition,
     Do not forget your life journey is journey of your
        feeling flow.

871. Your strength, your patience, your passion are
        unmatched,
     Set out imagining, dreaming and initiating yourself
        into action,
     No one can stop you, the ultimate victory is yours.

872. Achieve, be content and share your happiness,
     The giver, not the taker, will be in high spirits,
     Friendship with your spouse is Heaven for you.

873. Overcome obstacles and you can conquer fear,
     If you try to give shape to your words you will
        become a writer,
     Look at acting as acting you can be the monarch of
        acting.

874. Curiosity can take you to distances,
     Fearlessness will take you to many places,
     Cultivate everything from hypothesis to your
         theory.

875. Study the logic which cautions you as well as
         encourages,
     If you guess about obstacles easy to overcome
         them,
     Don't you ever underestimate the results of your
         work.

876. Forgive them, but do not forgive their wrongs,
     There is danger if you refuse to face evil boldly,
     Pat the back of good and break the back of bad,
         winner you will be.

877. Will doing the same thing the same way result
         differently?
     Your naivety it is, shouldn't the method change to
         suit the situation,
     The work you do will not fail if you are careful.

878. For education and for doing good, there is no age
         limit,
     There are no limits, if your goal is social progress,
     No excuse of old age, move forward on the path of
         activity.

879. Karma marga,the path of action is not above
       discretion,
     Jnana Yoga is the ideational web which guides karma
     Bhakti Yoga is the web of Devotion guiding Dhyana
       marga.

880. Infinite imaginative power, do not care about others,
     Your shield of fearlessness will remove all hurdles,
     Choose the right path and win the vehicle of right
       mode.

881. Because the believer in the truth doesn't fib, he
       doesn't care,
     Words weighed and used cannot be misunderstood,
     If you overcome partiality and ingratitude, success
       is yours.

882. Know your limits, overcome them carefully,
     Identify those who seek your fall and beware of them,
     Find out who your benefactors are, and behave well
       with them.

883. Share your affection with everyone you are close to,
     Trust only some dependable ones, well no choice,
     Doing no harm to anyone brings good luck.

884. Choose properly, increase efficiency and be the
       Decider,
     There is no harm in deciding what to care for,
     Your choice, your ability and nature will help you
       out.

885. To see the rainbow look upwards and fix your sight,
For water purification look down and focus,
To achieve love, look straight and slide the sight.

886. Efficiency, courage, diligence are essential,
What is the point without an opportunity,
So focus on the creation of an opportunity.

887. The rude man and the barking dog will cool down if
you stand up,
Add collated data to the hypothesis and research is
the fruit,
Your students will shine because of your invaluable
encouragement.

888. Nutritious food and also work nourish the body,
The quality and quantity of food is worth keeping
your eyes on,
Your interest is more important than the size of the
workspace.

889. Eliminate anger, exorcise negativity,
Forgive and coordinate the path of harmony,
Achieve what is intended, everyone can share the
fruits.

890. If anger becomes fury with revenge motive, it is
suicidal,
If okay for now, achieve reconciliation and good
will result.
No revenge, no ill will, and forgiving will end well.

Vennelakanti Prakasam

891. The weight of responsibilities brings you name and
        fame,
      If carried well, dignity stays and no dearth of glory,
      The Divine path is in the execution itself.

892. Opportunities for good deeds are plenty in hard
        times,
      Rains provide the needed support for the crops and
        dairying,
      With the investment of right words you can reduce
        resentment and enmity.

893. If done well not to be worried about anyone and
        anything,
      There should be no undue demand, nor undue
        negligence,
      For right results desire and detachment blend well.

894. Start your activity with what is required,
      Then access what is possible and continue with
        your work,
      You cannot totally avoid to peeping in of the
        impossible.

895. Sliding the sight between spouses should be a daily
        ritual,
      Be sure the sweetest experiences are in the net of
        love,
      This is all for the two of you and not for others, be
        sure.

896. True wisdom does not allow anger to germinate,
    Enough if one of you is smart to have harmony,
    There should be just love between spouses, not
        competing ownership.

897. 'How beautiful! your dress has acquired part of it,'
    'How long will you keep looking at me?'
    Such sentences should be heard frequently between
        spouses.

898. Marriage is the bond that binds friendship which is
        inseparable,
    Competitiveness is weak and you want to be strong,
        right?
    Pray for yourself in any religious frame,you will
        shine.

899. Swing in the flow of love, dutifulness is also love,
    Draw your relatives close to you, mistakes should
        be forgiven,
    Know that your behaviour is the ideal for your
        children.

900. Friednship is strengthened when minds are close,
    Excel each other in strengthening the bond of
        friendship,
    Adjust to each other's shortcomings and become
        one, be smart!

901. Do not forget that you are for each other,
     Contributing husband and the parenting wife are
          equals,
     Weak think more of themselves, you be strong and
          think of each other

902. Love, patience and piety make you one,
     Do what you can and increase your income,
     Run the kitchen without relying on others.

903. Do not blame one another for spending, silence is
          good,
     Both must be aware of the budget and its limits,
     The ideas can be given later as suggestion, be nice
          to each other.

904. Spouse is the partner who ripens life,
     Weddings are for fun and for seasonal employment,
     Marriage is for children and adults,

905. Marriage is another name for alliance reciprocalle,
     Without being asked they fulfil each other's needs,
     The two must jel together to make others happy.

906. The hardest of all difficulties is the lack of trust in
          other's words,
     Avoid telling lies as much as possible, just fib or be
          smilingly silent,
     Value facts, speak truth and be gracefully
          compliant.

907. Lies between spouses are heinous atrocities,
There are no greater friends than spouses,
Do not seek refuge in lies, the drink of truth is the
right refuge.

908. Less difficult it is to convert penury into plenty,
Learning words is also not too difficult,
Do not give place to hatred, it is very difficult to
change.

909. Can extinguish fire, can settle debt,
Can get praise, can get lentils,
Correcting a mistake is a bit too difficult, beware!

910. Let not hope evaporate, if support is needed in
hard times,
Don't let down courage, it matters a lot to achieve
anything,
Do not give up saving, it comes to our rescue in
hard times.

911. Do not own negativity, otherwise resist,
Nourish positivity, the community will benefit,
Society will benefit,families thrive and individuals
grow.

912. Change is natural, skill is essential,
Difficulties do change, all work demands skill,
Feeling of plenty is more important than wealth.

                                   Vennelakanti Prakasam

913. Your style of facing difficulties is yours,
Don't forget that method, it's yours
Difficulty is natural, needs facing, your method is
    unique.

914. Laziness deserves forgiveness in the summer,
But keep up intellection, write a little,
Survival is difficult if thinking is closed.

915. Appropriate work should be done by the disabled,
It is important to provide work for the unemployed,
Free food damages self esteem and man hours are lost.

916. Do not let pessimism come anywhere near,
Only mentally ill people are eligible for assistance,
Working is people's duty, providing work is
    government's duty.

917. Manual work energises but seeks strength,
Mental work seeks subject knowledge,
Manual or mental, fruits should reach others.

918. The difficulty of the non worker is detrimental to
    the body and mind,
Favoured work will yield fruit in some form or the
    other,
Congruent activity yields appropriate results.

919. Writing work and preaching work,
Mental they are, but leisure activities,
Lazy inactivity is a disaster for the being.

920. If idle fellow gets into addictions, dangerous it is,
Inaction does not fit in, worker's right activity is of
value,
Prayers, entertainment and creations are all good
work.

921. Food production, shelter building and fabric making,
Know them as basic and give full financial support,
Other things are necessary but they are not primary,

922. The main wealth is the result of the primary good
deeds,
On these depend the social life, true indeed,
Other treasures also are based on primary wealth.

923. Work not yielding recognized fruit is not
productive work,
Work yielding unrecognized fruit is not niche work,
Work must be fruitful and also widely useful for
others.

924. Delivery of goods to various places is work,
Unpaid work, even as services, is work,
Destroying what exists is bad, but work.

925. The task of eradicating evil is work done by the
government,
Violence for profit is bad,counter violence to curb
it, all work.
Violence of a bigot and counter violence of a victim
are all work.

926. Violence, retaliation, punishment, factionalism and
          revenge are all work,
      But the things that generate wealth constitute the
          real work,
      And the reward for the true doer should be adequate.

927. Community protection and national defence are
          work,
      Along with the production, protection IS
          important,
      It is not work to show people the wrong path with
          deceitful speeches.

928. Hate speech against strangers is not a chore,
      Misdemeanor is not inaction but it is bad work,
      You have to promote good deeds by kniving the evil
          deeds.

929. Valuable vehicle for socialness is the spousal bond,
      Valuable vehicle for acquisition of knowledge is
          education,
      Valuable vehicle for active consciousness is virtuous
          unity.

930. Impatience is a symbol of ignorance, education is
          what we grasp,
      It is natural to want what is conceived to happen in
          reality,
      It is criminal to resort to violence for something
          that did not happen.

931. True love does not jolt nor does it discriminate,
      Everyone is like you, so all are coevals,
      Coevals brook no rivalry, only comraderie.

932. May the waves of compassion move in your smile,
      May the warmth of our feeling be in your smile,
      Let the feeling of support in your smile shine well.

933. Let not the internet make us its prisoners,
      Let the internet broaden our perspective,
      Use it as much as you need and glow as a cosmopolitan.

934. Universal oneness is the Divine path,
      Achieve the concept of oneness, and stay with it,
      Measure the Divinity within you and seek salvation.

935. You are a knower if you can see manyness in oneness,
      You are knower when you can see oneness in
          manynesss,
      Divinity is the integrity of the individual and the
          universe.

936. The giver and the receiver are part of the cosmos,
      The angry man's vision slows down, forgive him,
      The only cure for him is calm words, not angry
          response.

937. Your fimness is a reflection of your strength,
      Your harshness is a sign of lack of tact,
      Tie tact with energy, sustenance and gratification
          will result.

                                    Vennelakanti Prakasam

938. Increase the sweetness and goodness in your speech,
      Gentleness and coolness of your gaze will spread
          your goodness,
      The feeling of brotherhood in thinking will achieve
          equality.

939. Divinity knows no creed, no caste and no region,
      Divinity recognizes all living beings as of one ilk,
      Achieving oneness is Heaven and disparateness is
          Hell.

940. All scriptures are sacred if properly understood,
      No scripture demands trusting without knowing
      Universal sense is more important than language.

941. If good sense prevails in them words are great,
      Great profit in actions if received by all,
      The real yoga is the skill in your activity.

942. Message is universally important but the
          messenger's name is not,
      The sanctity of practising method is more
          important than actual success,
      Failure is success when there is attention and
          aspiration.

943   Character is more important than literacy and
          counting,
      The fabric should be more weather-friendly than of
          flashy colour,
      The symbol of racial affiliation without universality
          is falsehood.

944. No final word for thought, no end to success,
Failure is not mortal, rethinking is not foolishness,
Try again, effort also is a stepping stone to success.

945. Do not rely on others for ideas and support,
Your consciousness, discretion and deliberation are
enough,
The real source of the investment needed for
business is thinking.

946. Concentrate your attention on the new rather than
the old,
Desire to take up what you can, not what you
cannot,
Increase the work size as your work progresses.

947. Do not blindly believe the words of others, weigh
them and take,
Handle business within the desired range, not for
show and fame,
Weigh the pros and cons, plan carefully and move
forward.

948. Truthfulness is more important than anything,
Profit making is fair but creating employement is of
greater value,
Creation of employment is more important than
the size of turnover.

949. The comprehensive awareness of the work you do is
          the first step,
      The identity of beneficiaries of that work and their
          needs is the second,
      The ambition to do is the third, the group who can
          do it is the last.

950. Complete awareness, the nature of recipients,
          strong desire and expertise,
      The edifice of your work stands on these four
          pillars,
      Investment comes along from somewhere from
          someone.

951. Do not worry, competitors are your coevals,
      Believe that the finished item can be changed if
          needed,
      The users' grumbling response will be your useful
          guide.

952. You will benefit from the torturing ideas of yours,
      Recognize and follow the edifice that is in your
          mind,
      Ideation, vision, perseverance are the real
          investment.

953. In leadership, many subleaders need to grow,
      A neat plan emerges from the labyrinth of opinions,
      That plan is your idea, your vision is your tool.

954. What is important is not what is read but what is
      learned,
   Believe, recognize, and respect your learning,
   Strengthen that learning to achieve success.

955. Be cautious, don't get scared, fib, do not lie,
   Courage and determination are needed but not
      hazards,
   If ideated, think you've got it, and proceed forward.

956. Do not feel small, do not denigrate others, praise if
      you like,
   Identify, analyse, correct your lapses to achieve full
      clarity,
   Accept positivity, nurture it and enhance it to
      strengthen yourself.

957. Logic is the base, the edifice is imagination-based,
   Progress with industriousness and get good results,
   Encourage your companions taking them as your
      own,

958. You must use your database very methodically
   What you ideate, verbalise and implement is your
      strength,
   Fill in your fellow worker's self-esteem and his
      determination.

959. Gather and analyze the opinions of others and
          decide,
      Do give your views if asked for on a particular
          subject,
      Your views are filled with the oxygen of your
          imagination.

960. Failure is actually awareness guide to success,
      Its causes are more important than failure itself,
      More important than success is an understanding
          of its process.

961. Smiling face is welcome for a wise man, not
          annoyance,
      Generosity suits the mother-in-law, not jealousy,
      Inflexibility doesn't become teachers, but openness
          does.

962. Education for knowledge is a multifaceted investment,
      Unsparing effort is the right tool for success,
      Peace is the key to the well-being of the people.

963. Education is not the right thing if you can't stand
          change,
      If it is not for the welfare of others why any position
          of power?
      Why support someone who is not ready to work?

964. Who is the instructor beyond the mind?
      Who is the saviour beyond the body?
      Who is the charioteer beyond the intellect?

965. The path that society has given us for education is
      school,
    Education is the way we choose to acquire
      knowledge,
    Knowledge is the tool we use for social welfare.

966. It is true that education is a mystical secret wealth,
    That wealth can have value only if it is for social
      welfare,
    What we do for ourselves is not work, same with
      wealth.

967. What can an uncommunicative teacher do for the
      children?
    How can unmoving wealth be uselful to society at
      large?
    Whatever is not useful for people is totally
      worthless.

968. If properly skilled, you can go upstream,
    Endurance can endure no matter how hard,
    A change-welcoming person can achieve growth.

969. Enthusiastic and encouraging help can nourish
      talent,
    Such talented people are capable of learning any
      subject,
    Giving students all kinds of training is the right
      thing to do.

                              Vennelakanti Prakasam

970. What is heard must not harm what is existent,
The new comers should not bring down the value
of the present staff,
Givers should never infringe on takers' self-esteem.

971. Not enough to know about subjects while studying,
Depths of life and socialness details are to be
comprehended,
Sources of Divinity can be guessed because of our
education.

972. Derive the conceptual bell from the dictionary
With grammar knowledge of knitting is clear,
Concepts and their bond structure need to be
understood.

973. Cause-effect relation, seed-field relation,
Relationship to dutifulness and detachment,
Only when you grasp all these true wisdom dawns.

974. Seeing what is thought of is not a big deal,
The merit of measuring its value is the deal,
Creating value for what is conceived is a deal.

975. Questioning for public praise is not a virtue,
Questioning for eradication of injustice is virtue,
Assisting with job creation along with free facilities
is virtue.

976. Ignorance does not belong to anyone, we should
        drive it away,
    Wisdom does not belong to anyone, we have to
        distribute it,
    It is no one's right to make a mistake, we have to
        resist it.

977. The new way of doing good survives,
    Logic-driven and action-easy advice surivives,
    Any good plan to help others survives.

978. The adaptation to the conditions of the nations is
        zeitgeist,
    Any welfare programme being conducive to
        progress is virtue,
    A king or a leader cannot neglect the welfare of the
        people.

979. Duty doing, peacekeeping and public welfare,
    This trident is important for any government,
    Inherited, elected or captured power cannot ignore
        the trident.

980. Destroy the building with falsity of foundation,
    Strengthen the building with truth as its
        foundation,
    The foundation of truth gives us the right path to
        achieve dharma.

     Vennelakanti Prakasam

981. Tradition is not a passive theory but a dynamic one,
      The building's foundation should stand when
          something is added,
      The past can be continued in the present form with
          necessary changes.

982. Do not be intimidated, do not threaten, just let the
          duty be done,
      Adding to the errors list is an ongoing processs,
      What is needed is the well-being of the talented
          people.

983. Wealth production is waste when requirements are
          not met,
      Wisdom is waste if the darkness of ignorance is not
          dispelled,
      Writings will be waste if they do no enlighten the
          readers.

984. Divine love is in you if you are a pacifist,
      Divine love is in you if you feel that everyone is
          yours,
      Divine love is in you if your chosen work gives you
          contentment.

985. Remember good health is a divine gift,
      Satisfaction in life is your divine wealth,
      Full faith is the divine bond in you.

986. Think of the feelings you have as Divine symbols,
Think of the feelings that light up in you as Divine
messages,
Let the lotus of your heart open up and receive the
Divine rays.

987. Divinity is described in different ways by different
Messengers,
These are parallel descriptions but not descriptions
of competition,
Visualise the Divine form with your own personal
cognizance.

988. It is not Divinity to regard peers as competitors,
It is not Divine to slander fellow humans,
It is not Divinity to buy comrades with three W's.

989. Be honest, be benevolent, be impartial all the
time,
Dutifulness, right actions, prevention of evil deeds
are imperative,
Know these are all the products of the Divine
formulae,

990. Selflessness should accompany prayer and
devotion,
Truth is imperative to reveal the Divine,
Dedicate your thinking for societal upkeep.

 Vennelakanti Prakasam

991. Socialness is goodwill above all else,
      Forgiveness is a virtue above all else,
      Compassion, Dutifulness and Agape are all
          supreme virtues.

992. Discover the concept of Divinity inherent in
          different cultures,
      Embrace the Divinity that is formed in your mind,
      You are the creator of your own sense of Divinity.

993. Universal Messages are for you to ponder,
      Universal Messages are to be remembered and
          recollected,
      Universal Messages are to provide you all kinds of
          longanimity.

994. The Sunrise gives you longanimity,
      The Sunset will bring you tranquillity,
      The Sun rays give you vitality and guide you forward.

995. Words said with compassion energise plants,
      Actions reflecting compassion are a great source
          for human advancement,
      Don't let negative feelings get into you and hurt
          other beings.

996. Change the objective if the expected results haven't
          come in,
      Change the path that did not reach the intended
          place,
      But don't you give up everything and slide off.

997. Never forget the Divine power within you,
      Share the Divine wisdom within you with others,
      Measure properly the Divinity within you.

998. No 'who for whom', know all for all,
      'Who should I strive and strain for', it is all for all,
      We must recognize the good and distribute the
          good to all.

999. Observe the world and discover its nature,
      Realize your nature and choose the path of karma,
      Your nature and surroundings will show you the
          destination.

1000. Seek Morale, Speak Morale and Live for Morale,
      Listen and understand the Universal Messages
          well,
      Imbibe the Messages and strengthen your Morale.

1001. Identify the concepts that come to your mind.

1002. Identify the services required for others.

1003. Identify the value of your task management.

1004. Try to share with others the good in you.

1005. Assume family responsibilities are Divine
          responsibilities.

1006. Recognize grace and charm everywhere and seek
          grace and charm.

1007. Perceive your goodwill and righteousness as
        Divine service.

1008. Eat with Contentment,See with Glow,Move with
        Friendship,Live with Love.

Epilogue

Here we present in detail the five principles mentioned in the prologue.

1. Socialness:

Society is linked with the individual. Unless the individuals come together society cannot form. Without society, the individual doesn't get identity, values, responsibilities and rights. This inseparable relationship achieves reciprocity. An individual becoming part of a community means owning many 'I's' as 'we' and treating others as the extended self. This is called spiralling self.

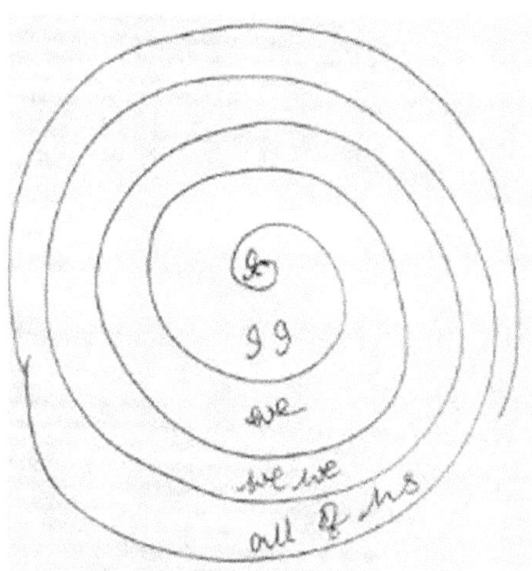

Here the differences of 'me' and 'others' disappear. This actually is the summative philosophy of most religious and political ideological strands.

An Individual's hunger, his neighbour's hunger, his worker's hunger, his health, his neighbour's health, his worker's health are one and the same. That kind of feeling is ideal. No one is put to any loss and no one faces any hardship. As an individual seeks proper wages for his work, he will have to see that others get proper wages for their hard work. Giving inadequate wages is generally called 'surplus labour'. One can also refer to it as 'labour theft'. This kind of labour theft is an enemy to socialness. We enjoy food, clothing, shelter, educational facilities and hospital facilities according to our capacity. It will be imperative for the haves to share the comforts with others in some form or other because it is the others who provide the basic comforts to the haves. If we deny such kind of sharing with society we are indulging in 'wealth theft'. Wealth theft and labor theft have to be avoided.

The Holy Quran says:

> "He rewards those who do evil according to their deeds
>
> And He rewards those who do good with what is best"(53-31)

This kind of doing evil and doing good are with reference to the actions of an individual towards other members of the society. If an individual refrains from wealth theft and labor theft besides practising social-ness correctly, the individual is on the virtuous track.

We have got to be respectful and affectionate to our parents and to our neighbours. Whatever services society expects us to render to others will have to be done. Besides refraining from wealth theft, we should never try to grab the property of orphans pretending to be taking care of them. We should not indulge in cheating with measurements and weights. We should not pretend to be knowing what we don't know. We should not develop wrong feelings of greatnes. All these messages are given in the 17th chapter of Holy Quran. In other words we are clearly told that we should refrain from not only wealth theft and labour theft but also from service theft and knowledge theft. We end up as thieves if we take what is not ours and if we don't give others what is theirs. Mind you what is theirs is not just money;it is respect, love, service etc.

A human being's wealth is not just money. His right to education, his right to health, his right to religious function, his right to respectful status, his right to be heard, his right to be properly recognized are all his wealth and no one has a right to thieve any aspect of his wealth.

If for some physical or mental reason some people cannot be equal to us it is our duty to share with them what we have. This is the base for socialness. Not doing it or ignoring it is a kind of wealth theft. Haves should join hands with have-nots. This strengthens socialness.

Greed is the trigger for labor theft. Negligence becomes cause for wealth theft. Labor theft and wealth theft both make society a furnace of hardships. Individuals on their own should contribute to the value of the society. The guiding authority evolved in society should become a guiding force for socialness. It is the duty of the affluent to see that penury doesn't get affected by meekness. If it keeps distance from complacency and arrogance it will befriend penury. Manusmruthi (Chapter 11) advices people not to ignore one's own family and parents while paying all attention to others' needs. The Holy Bible (Mathew 15) strongly advises us look after our parents.

Gautama Buddha says that we should develop a positive orientation towards society with a clean mind and a friendly heart without any ill will (Maha Seehanadha sutra).

The Holy Quran wants us to the pay the worker appropriate wages and instantly and the same thing is mentioned by Manusmriti. All these are part of our commitment to socialness. Manusmriti and Quran both condemn using deceptive weapons, and fighting and killing the ones who surrender and who are unarmed.

The Jewish tradition says that the farmers should leave the crop close to the fencing unreaped so that it can be used by the poor and the animals. All these are supporting socialness and wealth sharing, not wealth thieving. The Holy Quran says that debtor should be given enough time and it would be much better if the debt is totally waived. This also is in support of socialness and wealth sharing.

If we can recognize common dignity in all, the humanness will get fortified. Marxism very strongly recommends the elimination of difference between manual work and mental work. As a result the main source of modern inequality in society will disappear. Mental work, whether philosophical discourse or mythological discourse and academic discourse, and physical work of immediate fruit-bearing or long range fruit-bearing we have got to give them adequate appreciable importance and pay accordingly. Only then we can say we have coronated socialness not an individual or investment. Only then we can say wealth theft and social theft have not taken place. There is another serious enemy to socialness, viz., hedonism, which ignores morality, authenticity, justice and righteousness and goes in for personal luxurious life style. Hedonism takes selfishness to its peak. Physical indulgence is the ultimate goal of this philosophy. It doesn't think of others' needs. In the process it hurts others' self respect and their well being. This kind of negative act can be called 'Moral theft'.

This hedonist path is the root cause of all sins. We should be guided by the fruit of discussion to subvert the aggressive postures of hedonism. We can always take either directly or indirectly the ideas propagated by religious and socio-political ideologies.

2. Dutifulness:

An individual has to perform certain duties to enjoy the social and societal values. What we do for ourself is not work. What we do for others as members of our society is work. These others may be kinsmen or may be distantly known people but one should remember all of them share the same consciousness. Eating, sleeping, bathing and spousing are not work. Cooking for oneself is not work. Cooking for others is work. To have a shower is not a work. Giving a shower is work. Reading a book to while away time or to prepare for an examination is not work. On other hand teaching others and preparing for that teaching is work. That's why we are paid wages for it. From cleaning the streets to ruling from the palace is work. When we agree to do some work that is our duty. In that duty is inbuilt a desire to do it. That is the work we agree to do. When we are forced to do something which we don't like that becomes drudgery. When we do something which we like and that bears fruit we feel happy.

The successful completion of work demands attention and concentration. If patience also comes in there is no place for anxiety, boredom and feeling of torture. That is the real Nishkama Karma, which can be defined as a self-fulfilling action characterized by ebullience. In one sense the doer is responsible only for the doing of the work;he cannot be responsible for either successful completion or non successful completion of the work. He cannot be given either credit or debit for the work done or not done. The crucial suggestion in this context is to be free from the ownership of the result.

Transcending the dualities of success or failure, friend or foe, bad and good etc is the key factor in achieving Emancipation or Liberation or Jeevanmukti. This is what Bhagavadgita says in Chapter-2 Slokas thirty eight and forty seven:

> (38) "Treat alike happiness and unhappiness, gain and loss, victory and defeat. Then start the battle and acting thus you will not incur any sin"

> (47)"Your authority is only to perform action, fruit thereof is not in your authority. Don't be a motive-driven actor, nor should you seek nonperforming action"

Doing your duty with skill and care is yoga. While doing one's duty, while following religious duties, or while performing acts of charity, there should not be an iota of pomposity or desire to show off. The Holy Bible is specific on this point (Matthew 6:1-4):

> "Take good care not to practise your righteousness in front of people in order to be observed by them."

> "When you go making gifts of mercy, do not blow a trumpet ahead of you."

> "When making gifts of mercy, do not your left hand know what your right is doing."

> "..your gifts of mercy may be in secret; then your Father who is looking on in secret will repay you."

These great ideas tell us that there should be *Sattvikata* (Righteousness) in our performance of action and also a bit of *Rajasikata* (firmness) too but not *Tamasikata* (indolence).

From the elementary school to the university, the teachers have only one duty: distribution of knowledge. Their vehicles, buildings, wealth and the like have no value. Students, their parents and also the Supreme Subjective Reality, God, do not give value to the property of the teachers. The salaries they get are fixed fruits of action. Wages they are. The real value the happy teachers enjoy is the acquisition of knowledge, creation of knowledge, sharing of knowledge and guiding demeanour. Nothing more.

In that great event of lifting of Govardhanagiri, Srikrishna turned the attention of the seekers from Yajnamarga to Jnanamarga and Karmamarga. Very significant point to note here is that Yajnamarga was of the few, by the few and for the few. On the other hand the twin margas of Jnana and Karma were for all, to be followed by all and happily belonging to all. This was the first great step to achieve Social Justice, curbing labour theft and wealth theft.

Similar is the content of the Purohit's advice to the King Mahavijita, mentioned by Gautama Buddha (Kutadanta Sutra:11):

"Please distribute fodder and grains to your subjects who grow crops and who rear cattle. Give capital

                                          Vennelakanti Prakasam

investment to your businessmen. Arrange right salaries to the government employees. In that case, the ones pursuing their profession will not contemplate any harm to you. Your income goes up. The Kingdom will be in plenitude. There will be no fear of thieves. People will all be very happy and satisfied, playing with their children. There will be no need for the people to close the doors of their houses."

This advice is applicable to all the administrative rulers, whether a King, President, Prime Minister, Governor, or a Chief Minister. It is the duty of the citizen to pay taxes in time:"Pay back, therefore, Caesar's things to Caesar, but God's things to God" (Matthew 22:21).Similarly the haves are expected to help the have-nots,feed the hungry, fulfill the needs of neighbours and it is part of their duty.

3. Love (Agape).

Agape is, like Higher Reality, Higher Love, the Love between God and the Human. It is free from possessiveness, envy, jealousy, and ownership feeling. Actually it is difficult to visualize, realize and define God and Agape (Divine Love/Divya Prema).It has to be distinguished from Erose (erotic love), and Philia (friendly love) and also from philautia (self-love), Storge(familial love), Ludus(playful love), Pragma (committed love). Pure lust may not come close even to erose.

We should become aware of love. We should experience love. We should share love only then humanity blooms. Human beings will become divine humans if they recognize the divine spirit in them which is also called consciousness. This divine spark is there in all beings.If a human being becomes aware of that spark in one and all, the difference of self and the other will vanish. We develop positive thinking about everyone. When Jesus said 'you must love your neighbor as yourself' (Mathew 22:39), and when he said 'continue to love your enemies and to pray for those persecuting you' (Mathew 5:44), we have to take it that he is asking us to see the Divine spirit in all the human beings. It is very important to remember that parents feel bad when their children quarrel and similarly the society will suffer if groups clash so we should have love for everyone. Here is another point to note. Let's say our enemy wishes us ill and we wish him ill. On other hand if we wish all well,no one is our enemy. If others wish us ill it is their negative attitude and their problem. We should not have a negative problem to pull us down.

Though it is not possible to give a comprehensive picture of love from all angles we can in a generalized way talk of three types of love. (1) The positive feelings we have towards society and other institutions we can call **self love** or **cosmic love**. When we say self love two points of signification emerge. The first one is that it has emanated in the self or it is properly stored in the self. The self has both physical and spiritual values. So the self no doubt remains in the self and thinks of itself but sees the similar self in others. So the cosmicness of love from the self is both centrifugal and centripetal.

(2) The love we have for people we know, our kith and kin.It is not only ideational but also practical. This kind of brotherhood love is of great importance. Because this brotherhood feeling is for all the fellow human beings, we can call it **societal love**. This is the love that vibrates in that primary requirement called socialness.

(3) The third type of love is the love which human being has reflecting his aptitude and aspirations. Mahabharat says that the bond that binds spouses is 'Sneham' (friendship). This sneham is **spousal love**. Men and women living together as life partners are characterized by this spousal love. This kind of love does not brook the pitfall of ownership. This is essentially an **alliance reciprocalle**. It doesn't brook the twin negatives of suspicion and doubt. The couples who understand that what flows between them is pure love will never have any problems. There will be only the feeling of darlingness. Similarly people have love for friends and things they like. This we can call **mundane love**. The ones who start with mundane love, go through societal love and end with cosmic love are the blessed folks. Such people do not suffer(from) hatred, fury, pomposity, hardheartedness, avarice and envy. Those beings of agape see themselves in others and see others in themselves and really enjoy the bliss of divine blessings.

4. Forgiveness:

The base for forgiveness is patience which is associated with tolerance. These two top qualities of Patience and Tolerance give us an extremely valuable tool called Forgiveness. Tolerating others' negativity and ignoring it are all possible if you have broad cognitive capability which many people refer to large-heartedness. For all this the base is what we called societal love which is midway between mundane and cosmic. Jesus Christ's guidance to us to forgive even the enemy comes from the general plea for love. Forgiving others, looking at their behaviour from different angles and ignoring it as their weakness, not as their bad intention. This kind of forgiving quality is not easily found in every individual and every family. The rulers have to take up the responsibility of controlling their region. For that one has to work from different angles. See what holy Quran says

> "Let not those among you
> Who are endued with grace
> And amplitude of means
> Resolve by oath against helping
> Their kinsmen, those in want,
> And those who have left
> Their homes for Allah's cause:
> Let them forgive and overlook"
>   (Surah 24:22 TR Abdullah Yusuf Ali).

The ability to forgive others is adornment for a strong man. There is nothing in this world you can't achieve with these twin blessings of love and forgiveness. No greater shield and No greater weapon. Forgiveness reflects the depth of our knowledge. It indicates our courage. Individuals may bear injustice done to them but injustice done to the society and damage done to the society may have to be taken care of appropriately with all the witness accounts.

5. Compassion

We may be doing our duty by being nice to fellow beings and also tolerating their lapses but it is necessary to pay attention to the weaker sections of society and also non human living beings. Compassion should be our compass. Look at what Jesus Christ said:

> "When you spread dinner or evening meal do not call your friends or your brothers or your relatives or rich neighbors. Perhaps sometime they might also invite you in return and would become a repayment to you. But when you spread feast, invite poor people, crippled, lame, blind; and you will be happy because they have nothing which to repay you, for you will be repaid in the resurrection of the righteous ones" (Luke 14:12-14).

What a beautiful example for the concept of compassion. Compassion is not for a reciprocal gesture. This kind of feast is Satvic feast. Rajasic feast is something we do as a return favor and with a little bit of display. Tamasic feast is for political purposes or other purposes which are not publicly acceptable.

Compassion is Satvic ardour. See what is said in Yogashastra a book of Jaina philosophy:

> "We should look after all the beings all the time and all the circumstances in all the situations the way we

look after our selves. We should not let any other being face what creates trouble for us. No violence should ever be inflicted on other beings".

Gautama Buddha says Prajna and Karuna are both important for enlightenment. Prajna (wisdom) causes compassion in us. Compassion helps us achieve wisdom. Interestingly it can be said wisdom and compassion are the constituents of enlightenment.

Others should not suffer. Such strong feeling is compassion, which seems to have both sympathy and empathy as its constituents along with a strong desire to alleviate the suffering of the other person. So compassion is kind of trident with Desire to Alleviate is the main strong blade, the other two blades connected to it are to help realize the depth of the problem are Sympathy and Empathy.

The blessed being endowed with love, compassion, forgiveness, dutifulness and socialness is Jeevan Mukta, the Liberated soul. This is the same as Sthitha Prajna described in Bhagavadgita (Chapter 12:13-19):

> 13 "One who hates no one, friendly with all and kind to all, Not possessive, Not arrogant, Sameness of pain and pleasure and who forgives."

> 14- "Always contented, Controlled, of Firm resolve,

> Surrendering mind and intellect to me such devotee is dear to me"

15- One of whom others are not tired and who is not tired of others, The one untouched by joy, anger, fear, discomfort that kind of man is dear to me.

16- A non-craving, pure, industrious, indifferent and undisturbed, Free from desirous actions that kind of devotee is dear to me.

17- Experiencing no joy, loathing nothing, regretting nothing and desiring nothing, Abandoning good or bad, the one with the devotion is dear to me.

18- Treating alike enemies and friends, honour and dishonour,

Heat and cold, pain and comfort and who is detached.

19- To whom praise and despisal are equal, quiet and contented, Someone with steady mind and desireless, that kind of devotee is dear to me.

To have compassion for fellow beings we should have agape, the cosmic love. We should be full of socialness feeling. Once with compassion, dutifulness will take its own place. Giving a shape to one's feeling is doing one's duty. Looking at all others as our reflections, transcending all dualities and leading peaceful life is liberation. This is Divine Bliss.